KU-183-600

CONTENTS

SYMBOLS KEY

The following is a key to the symbols used throughout this book:

ℹ️ information office	✈️ airport	⬡ fine dining
🚌 bus stop	🍴 restaurant	🛍️ shopping
✉️ post office	☕ café	↘️ tip
✝️ church	🍸 bar	

---

❶ telephone	❶ fax	ⓔ email	ⓦ website address
ⓐ address	🕐 opening times	❶ important	
€ budget price	€€ mid-range price	€€€ most expensive	
★ specialist interest	★★ see if passing	★★★ top attraction	

HOT
IBIZA

Thomas Cook

Written and researched by Mike Gerrard, updated by Jane Egginton
Front cover photography courtesy of Thomas Cook Tour Operations Ltd

Original design concept by Studio 183 Limited
Series design by the Bridgewater Book Company
Cover design/artwork by Lee Biggadike, Studio 183 Limited

Produced by the Bridgewater Book Company
The Old Candlemakers, West Street, Lewes, East Sussex BN7 2NZ, United Kingdom
www.bridgewaterbooks.co.uk
Project Editor: Emily Casey Bailey
Project Designer: Lisa McCormick

Published by Thomas Cook Publishing
A division of Thomas Cook Tour Operations Limited
PO Box 227, Units 15-16, Coningsby Road, Peterborough PE3 8SB, United Kingdom
email: books@thomascook.com
www.thomascookpublishing.com
+ 44 (0) 1733 416477

ISBN-13: 978-1-84157-536-0
ISBN-10: 1-84157-536-4

First edition © 2006 Thomas Cook Publishing
Text © 2006 Thomas Cook Publishing
Maps © 2006 Thomas Cook Publishing
Head of Thomas Cook Publishing: Chris Young
Project Editor: Diane Ashmore
Production/DTP Editor: Steven Collins

Printed and bound in Spain by Graficas Cems, Navarra, Spain

INTRODUCTION
Getting to know Ibiza

MEDITERRANEAN SEA

CAP

PORT DE SANT MIQUEL

SANT MIQUEL

SANTA

CALA GRACIÓ

SANT ANTONI
(SAN ANTONIO TOWN)

SANT RAFEL

CALA BASSA

PORT DES
TORRENT

SANT ANTONI BAY

CALA CONTA

CALA TARIDA

419m

EI

SANT JOSEP

475m

FIGUERET

CALA VADELLA

PLATJA D'EN

CALA D'HORT

ES CAVALLET

N

SES SALINAS
LA CANAL

0   5   10km
0   6 miles

Bay of Biscay

Atlantic Ocean

FRANCE

PORTUGAL

SPAIN

MALLORCA

IBIZA

FORMENTERA

Mediterranean Sea

MOROCCO

ALGERIA

PORTINATX

SANT JOAN

SANT VICENT

CALA SANT VICENT

10m

AIGUES BLANQUES

SANT CARLES

ES CANAR

S'ARGAMASSA

SANTA EULÀRIA (SANTA EULÀLIA)

CALA LLONGA

(OWN)

FORMENTERA

N

Mediterranean Sea

PORT DE LA SAVINO

ES PUJOLS

SANT FRANCESC

CALA SAONA

PLATJA DE MITJORN

ES CALÓ

EL PILAR DE LA MOLA

Playa de Mitjorn

Sa Talalassa (192m)

ES CAP DE BARBARÍA

0 1 2 3 4 5km

0   3 miles

Getting to know Ibiza (Eivissa)

Artists discovered it in the 1950s, hippies in the 1960s, the jet set in the 1970s, and by the 1990s it had become the biggest all-night party place in Europe. Welcome to Ibiza. This little jewel of an island is home to film stars and fishermen, farmers and fashion models, expats and tourists. You can be anything on Ibiza, but one thing you won't be is bored. You may see some outrageous things, but you can be sure that whatever they are, the people who live here have seen it all before.

All this takes place on an island about the size of the Isle of Man – but with rather a better climate! Ibiza boasts 300 sunny days a year, with ten hours of sunshine a day in the summer and even five hours a day most days in winter. The average August has 31 sunny days in a row, but that doesn't mean it never rains. Most of the rainfall saves itself for the October to December period, but even if there's a freak summer storm or shower, you know it won't last and it's never enough to dampen the spirits.

WHERE ARE WE?

As for the island itself, it's in the western Mediterranean and forms part of the Balearic Islands with neighbouring Mallorca (or Majorca) and Menorca. Ibiza and the much smaller isle of Formentera close by are known as the *Islas Pitiusas*, meaning the pine-covered islands. Ibiza is about 240 km (150 miles) south of Barcelona on the Spanish mainland, and about the same distance from Algiers on the North African coast. You'll probably notice an African influence in some of the buildings, while others are in the simple white cube style, similar to the Greek Island houses, at the eastern end of the Mediterranean.

WHAT LANGUAGE?

As with the Greek Islands, most people working in the popular tourist areas speak good English. However, a little Spanish goes a long way so try and master a few basics (see pages 119–120 for some useful words and phrases). Bear in mind that the people of Ibiza – the Ibicencos –

might speak Catalan, or they might speak their local dialect of Catalan, Ibicenco, or Castilian Spanish. All three languages exist side by side, which can be a little confusing until you get used to it. Road signs are usually in Catalan, but maps are often in Spanish, so be prepared for most places to have two slightly different names. Catalan names are used in this book for main resorts. The locals know their own island, and its main town, by the name of Eivissa.

THE REAL IBIZA

Whatever you call it, the island is beautiful. It has lots of lovely sandy beaches, some busy and others quiet and hidden away. Its highest point, Sa Talaia, may only be 475 km (1560 ft), but you can see the Spanish mainland if you venture to the top on a clear day. This peak is surrounded by some fertile farmland, some saltflats, and even that rare thing for a small Mediterranean island: a river. There are villages inland that are almost untouched by tourism, and you should definitely make an effort to explore the interior and meet the people who don't normally meet the tourists.

You'll get an incredibly warm welcome, especially if you venture into a village's only bar or café, or try to buy something in the solitary shop. This is what some people like to call 'the real Ibiza', though the truth is that everywhere on the island is now 'the real Ibiza', from hamlets that are sleepy to bustling resorts that are virtually sleepless.

PEOPLE & PLACES

About 100,000 people live on Ibiza, about 35,000 of them in the capital, usually known to holidaymakers as Ibiza Town. It's a lively place where everyone finds something to interest them, whether it's the old walled town, Dalt Vila, with its cathedral and museums, the ever-changing bar and club scene, the fishing harbour, the designer shops, the art galleries or the range of restaurants.

However long you think you'll need when you visit Ibiza Town – make it longer. And if you find you haven't had enough of Ibiza by the end of your holiday, you can always come back. Most people do.

The best of Ibiza

BEACHES

Most people come to Ibiza for two reasons: beaches and clubbing. Ask your rep for information about nights out. If you want to explore good beaches outside your own resort, here are some of the most popular: **Platja d'en Bossa** (page 21), **Cala Tarida** and **Cala d'Hort** (page 26), **Ses Salines**, **Cala Sant Vicent** (page 48) and **Es Canar** (page 53). On the island of Formentera (page 85), the **Platja de Illetes** is a spectacular white sand beach. **Ses Salines** has a small nudist section, nearby **Es Cavallet** is an unofficial gay nudist beach, plus there is **Aigües Blanques** (page 51) on the north-east coast.

AWAY FROM THE COAST

An organized island tour will take in the best beaches and show you some of the scenery of the interior. You'll discover why Ibiza and Formentera were known to Greek traders as 'the pine islands'. Alternatively, rent a car for a few days and see some of the unspoilt inland villages.

THE BEST OF THE REST

- No visit to Ibiza would be complete without wandering round the **Dalt Vila** in Ibiza Town, the medieval town within the ancient walls (page 18) a World Heritage Site since 1999.
- See **Santa Eulària** (page 63), Ibiza's third largest town which combines modern tourism with a traditional atmosphere.
- Take a day trip to **Formentera** (page 85), a much more peaceful island, which can be explored on a bike, local bus, by car, or on foot.
- Few people need encouraging to try *paella* and *sangria*, but try squid and fresh fish too, and the local *hierbas*, a drink that combines alcohol with herbs.
- Visit **Ibiza Town** at night, especially the **La Marina** district between the city walls and the port. You'll see a parade of people from the beautiful to the extraordinary.
- Take in one of the **hippy markets**. They are a great mix of locals, hippies, Africans and tourists: a good cross-section of Ibizan life, in fact.

RESORTS
Places under the sun

Ibiza Town
bustling island capital

A trip to Ibiza's capital, which combines the old city with the modern town, makes a great day out; you'll see a tremendous range of souvenirs and be spoilt for choice when it comes to eating out. The local name for it is Eivissa, and this is what you'll see on buses and road signs. You'll know when you're getting there, as you will see the high old town, Dalt Vila, clustered around its rock on top of which sits the cathedral.

There are several sights to see, if that's what you enjoy, but equally pleasant is simply to wander the streets of both Dalt Vila and the area known as La Marina. This stands between Dalt Vila and the port, and while busy with souvenir stalls and cafés during the day, it really buzzes at night when its bars and restaurants attract an eye-opening cast of characters.

If you come by bus, check the return times. Buses run until quite late, so you could plan to stay for dinner and have a few drinks here. You could even spend the evening shopping; most shops stay open until 23.00 hours in the old part of the town. Your resort representative can also offer a night tour of Ibiza Town.

THINGS TO SEE & DO
Boat trips ★★
There are all kinds of boat trips available from the port in Ibiza Town to beaches and to Marina Botafoch on the north side of the port. Spend a few hours visiting nearby bays or charter a yacht for up to 40 people in Marina Botafoch.

Dalt Vila ★★★
The old town should be high on everyone's list of options (see page 18). You're sure to get lost as you make your way through the zigzag streets climbing towards the cathedral, but that's part of the fun. On the way you will pass through the Portal de Ses Taules, the main gateway through the

city walls, completed in 1585. Sit at any one of the many cafés or bars around the port or the nearby tiny streets and watch the world go by. Just about any time of the day or night there is plenty going on. You can take a waterside walk through the port, or take a short boat ride to Botafoch Marina and see Dalt Vila floodlit across the water at night.

Puig des Molins ★

The Hill of the Windmills, next to Dalt Vila doesn't have as many windmills as before but there are archaeological excavations. The museum is closed for long-term renovations but the necropolis is open. Several thousand Carthaginian tombs have been found here. The Carthaginians ruled the island from 654–146 BC. ❷ Vía Romana 31 ❶ 971 30 17 71 ◕ Open Tues–Sun 10.00–13.30 and Tues–Fri 17.00–20.00

◑ *Ibiza Town (also known as Eivissa)*

IBIZA NUEVA MARIN
MARINA BOTAFO

AV. IGNASI WALLIS

C. DE VICENT SERRA ORVAY

AV. BARTOMEU DE ROSELLÓ

AV. D'ISIDORO MACABICH

AV. D'ISIDORO MACABICH

C. JOAN D'AUSTRIA

AV. BARTOMEU VICENT RA

C. DE MADRID

C. DE CASTELLA

C. DEL BISBE HUI

PASSEIG V

EGLÉSIA DE
SANTA CREU

Sa Capelleta

NEW
MARKET

VIA PUNICA

AV. ESPANYA

VIA ROMANA

MUSEU I
NECRÒPOLIS

Puig des
Molins

● *Ibiza Town*

SHOPPING

Club Wear All the major clubs have shops along the port.

Fashion/Jewellery Again, La Marina is the place to look. In addition, there are more shops in Dalt Vila, most of them near to the Plaça de Vila.

Mango The same good-quality clothes you'd find in Mango shops at home, but cheaper. ⓐ Carrer Riambau ⓛ Open 11.00–23.00

Markets An evening hippy market takes place in La Marina. The fruit and fish market near the bus stops (ⓛ Open until 14.00), is worth a visit – ask for *el mercado*.

RESTAURANTS (see map on pages 14–15)

As you wander around the port and the narrow streets of the marina area, there are plenty of bars and restaurants to choose from. During the day look out for the economical fixed-price menu, *menú del día*, in the new part of town.

Formentera €€ **1** One of the oldest restaurants in Ibiza, serving the best of island cooking and international dishes. **a** Plaça de La Tertulia 5 **t** 971 31 10 24 **o** Open 13.00–16.00 and 19.00–00.30

La Raspa €€€ **2** Fantastic views from the terrace to Dalt Vila. Inside, the restaurant is decorated like a boat and it has its own tank of lobsters. **a** Marina Botafoch, local 205 (other side of the harbour) **t** 971 31 18 10 **o** Open 20.30–01.00

Los Valencianos € **3** Join the locals at this home-made ice cream parlour. Sit on the large terrace and watch the world go by. Ideal for children and non clubbers. **a** Near the marina **o** Open noon–01.00

NIGHTLIFE

Stroll along the harbour and have a look at the luxury cruisers. You will get a good view of the parades advertising the clubs from any of the bars in the port. For something different, try **Bar Pereira** – good for live music – jazz or soul (**a** Just off Passeig Vara de Rey **t** 971 31 04 09 **o** Open every night).

Casino de Ibiza is just a short boat ride from the port across the harbour to the Ibiza Nueva Marina. As well as gaming rooms, there is a restaurant jackpot, which serves a variety of international dishes as well as pizza (**a** Passeig Joan Carles I **t** 971 31 33 12 **w** www.casinoibiza.com **o** Restaurant open 21.00–03.00; gambling open 17.00–06.00).

El Divino and **Pacha** are two popular clubs across the harbour near the Ibiza Nueva Marina (**w** www.eldivino-ibiza.com **w** www.pacha.com **o** Open midnight–07.00).

Dalt Vila
walled medieval town

The medieval town of Dalt Vila sits like a crown above Ibiza Town. Within its ancient walls are several museums and a cathedral as well as shops and restaurants. It's a great place to wander – just let yourself get lost along the tiny twisting alleys.

One of the best ways to explore this area is to take either a taxi (ask the driver for 'Es Soto') and walk down, or use the 'vila bus' from Vara de Rey to the top. It is worth doing this to avoid walking up the steep inclines that can be especially tiring in the heat of the day. There are great views of the town and out to sea from here. Access by car is for residents only.

THINGS TO SEE & DO
Museu Arqueològic de Dalt Vila (Archaeological Museum) ★
Worth seeing if you're interested in the history of Ibiza and Formentera, with good displays and explanations in English. ⓐ Next to the cathedral ⓣ 971 30 12 31 ⓔ maef@telefonica.net ⓛ Open Tues–Sat 10.00–14.00 and 18.00–20.00, Sun 10.00–14.00 ⓘ Admission charge

Catedral de Santa María (Cathedral) ★
It is thought that there has been some kind of temple on this site for at least 2500 years. Parts of the present building, such as the bell tower, date from the 14th century, but most are from the 18th. Opposite the cathedral is the castle, currently closed to the public owing to its dilapidated interior. ⓐ Plaça Catedral ⓛ Open Tues–Sat 10.00–13.00, Mass Sun 10.30, closes after mass

Museu d'Art Contemporani (Museum of Contemporary Art) ★
A very small collection, but it has temporary exhibitions which change every two months. ⓐ Ronda Narcis Puget ⓣ 971 30 27 23 ⓛ Open Tues–Sun 10.00–13.30 and Tues–Fri 17.00–20.00, closed Mon ⓘ Admission charge

Plaça d'Espanya ★

This pleasant square on the edge of Dalt Vila contains a statue of Guillem de Montgri, a captor of the island in 1235. The large Town Hall here was originally a monastery, of which the church of Santo Domingo still stands.

Wear flat, comfortable shoes for exploring the medieval streets of Dalt Vila, as they are cobbled and very steep.

RESTAURANTS (see map on pages 14–15)

La Oliva €€ ❹ This typically Mediterranean-style restaurant has a charming rustic interior as well as seating outside and is located in a quaint, narrow street just off Plaça de Vila. There's also the occasional street performer to add to your evening out. ⓐ Carrer Santa Creu 2 ❶ 971 30 57 52 ⓛ Open 19.30–01.00

El Olivo €€€ ❺ The splurge option if you want French cuisine, including fresh fish and fine seafood, in unique surroundings. ⓐ Plaça de Vila 8 ❶ 971 30 06 80 ⓛ Open 19.00–01.00, closed Mon ⓘ Worth booking in advance

La Plaza €€€ ❻ This is another upmarket restaurant, just inside the old town walls, serving fish and Spanish dishes. ⓐ Plaça de Vila 18 ❶ 971 30 76 17 ⓛ Open 20.00–midnight

🔺 *La Oliva in Dalt Vila*

Platja d'en Bossa & Figueretes
lively twin resorts

Platja d'en Bossa is one of the most popular resorts on the island. The main reason is that it has the longest beach on Ibiza – almost 3 km (2 miles) of gently shelving beach covered in fine white sand and backed by a fringe of palm trees –and rows of hotels, shops, bars and eating places that cater to the many visitors.

Families like it here because it's very safe for young children, while older ones can make use of the water sports facilities along the beach, such as windsurfing and water-skiing. Adults enjoy the nightlife, and the fact that it's very easy to get into Ibiza Town from here, for more nightlife and good shopping.

Between Platja d'en Bossa and Ibiza Town is the much smaller resort of Figueretes (the name means 'the little fig trees'), although they all tend to merge into each other these days. Figueretes has become popular with gay men, and has some bars and hotels. From here you can walk into Ibiza Town in 15 minutes.

Figueretes has a lovely promenade running along its length. Here you will find bars, cafés and restaurants to suit just about anyone.

TRANSPORT
There are buses running from stops throughout Platja d'en Bossa and Ibiza Town. There are also regular boats from the jetties between Platja d'en Bossa, Figueretes and Ibiza Town. There are taxi ranks next to both main beaches. **ⓦ** www.ibizabus.com

◀ *Platja d'en Bossa is popular for sailing and windsurfing*

THINGS TO SEE & DO

Aguamar Water Park ★★

This water park in Platja d'en Bossa is the perfect place to spend a day if you've got children, or even if you haven't. There are water-chutes like the Kamikaze and the Black Hole – not for the faint-hearted – and a bar and a restaurant, plus garden areas and a picnic area. ❶ 971 39 67 90 ❷ Open daily in summer 10.00–18.00

 If you're going to the Aguamar Water Park, bear in mind that you can get a re-entry pass and visit the beach opposite, so you can break up the day, and return later.

Cruise ★★

A glass-bottomed boat leaves Hotel Ibiza Playa on Figueretes beach twice daily for day trips to **Formentera** (see page 85).

Park ★

A small park near Figueretes, **Parc de la Pau**, is popular with locals and holidaymakers alike, with grass and a play area. ❷ Near the bus stop on Av. Isidoro Macabich (see map on page 39).

BEACHES

Platja d'en Bossa has the longest stretch of beach on the island, which shelves gently, so is good for young children. It is backed by bars and restaurants and there is a sailing and windsurfing school. The northern end tends to be a bit more peaceful. The beach at **Figueretes** is quite narrow, but pleasant, and a water-skiing school can be found here. To the south **Es Cavallet** is the famous nudist beach, and **Ses Salines** is also popular among party-goers. The saltflats nearby make for interesting walking as the whole area has been declared a nature reserve.

Beach parties Platja d'en Bossa is famous for its parties. **Bora Bora**, by the Jet Apartments, has a beach party most afternoons, while clubbers who've been up all night go from the after-party in **Space** nearby (see page 25).

◯ The beach at Platja d'en Bossa

RESTAURANTS & BARS

 Big Bens € A lively English bar, suitable for families. ⓐ Centre of Platja d'en Bossa ⓣ 971 30 59 71

 Bull Bar € Caters for all the family, with bouncy castles, a rodeo bull and other entertainment. ⓐ Between Bossa and Es Vive
🕐 Open noon–02.00

 Cafeteria America €€ Spanish with international cuisine. Set menus. ⓐ On the main promenade at Figueretes ⓣ 971 30 34 38
🕐 Open 11.00–23.00

 Chino Taiwan €€ Tasty Chinese dishes, generous portions and reasonably priced. ⓐ On the main promenade at Figueretes
ⓣ 971 30 16 19 🕐 Open 11.30–midnight

Insula Augusta €€ Right on the beach at Platja d'en Bossa, this makes a great place to have a lazy lunch, though it's open in the evenings too. ⓐ Southern end of beach ⓣ 971 39 08 82
🕐 Open noon–midnight

 Monroes Bar € Friendly place with home-made food and entertainment nightly. ⓐ Carrer Ramón Muntaner
ⓣ 971 39 25 41 🕐 Open 09.30–02.00

Murphy's Irish Bar € There's live music and draught Guinness at this bar-pub, which caters for children too. ⓐ Southern end of Platja d'en Bossa 🕐 Open 21.00–02.00

Principe €€ This place has a shady terrace and specializes in seafood, including lobsters and shellfish fresh from its own tanks.
ⓐ On the beach at Figueretes ⓣ 971 30 19 14 🕐 Open noon–01.00, Wed 18.00–01.00

SHOPPING

The area between Figueretes and Vara de Rey, in the old town, provides the main shopping centre for locals and tourists alike. ● Open Mon–Fri 09.00–13.30 and 17.00–20.00; some shops in this area close on Saturday afternoon.

The hippy market A great place to buy arts and crafts, T-shirts, jewellery and a good range of more conventional souvenirs. ● Platja d'en Bossa ● Open every Friday 11.00–20.00 hours

La Sirena A hypermarket on two floors close to the Aguamar Water Park with clothes, leather, ceramics and perfume at discount prices. ● 971 30 23 41 ● Open 09.00–19.00

Romana Mia €€ This Italian restaurant does pizza, pasta and fresh fish dishes. There is also a very reasonable set menu. ● On the sea over-looking the promenade at Figueretes ● 971 30 59 42 ● Open 10.00–01.00

NIGHTLIFE

Beach parties at the bars along the promenade are always lively and crowded. **Space** is the after-party place, though it hardly qualifies as nightlife as it doesn't open until 07.00 hours, and runs for 22 hours. Check for opening days, which change seasonally. ● www.space-ibiza.com

● Aguamar Water Park

Cala Tarida & Cala d'Hort
two tucked-away bays

There are some little gems of places in the south-west corner of Ibiza, and these are two of them. The first is a lively little resort, and the second a small and very popular cove with great views out to sea.

Cala Tarida doesn't have a huge beach but it's got lovely white sand and there's also plenty of sunbathing space on the rocks at both ends of the beach. It also shelves gently into the sea so is great for young children, and there are water sports facilities and pedalos for hire as well. A couple

○ *The gently sloping beach of Cala Tarida is great for young children*

of well-situated eating places look out over the beach and the sea, and in the little town above the beach there are several shops to provide your basic provisions.

Cala d'Hort is at the end of a steep, winding road, and is definitely worth making the effort to visit, although it can only be reached by taxi or private car. The beach is small and sandy, there are one or two shops and a couple of excellent beachside restaurants ... and that's it. It's a blissful place, and even if you're there when it's crowded it's still got great views.

Offshore are two islands, the huge one with steep cliffs is Es Vedrà and is said to have mystical powers. Cala d'Hort is the beach used in the filming of the Rodgers and Hammerstein musical *South Pacific.*

What you are more likely to see is a flock of the very rare Eleonora's falcons, which live in the nearby cliffs. There are only about 500 of these small birds of prey in the whole of the Mediterranean, and they're the only birds of prey which live in groups. Look in the early evening sky, if you can, to watch them flocking and catching insects.

Cala d'Hort is very busy, especially at weekends, and car parking space is limited. But you can drive down to the end of the road, check out the availability, and then easily turn round and return to park further back if you need to.

THINGS TO SEE & DO
Water sports ★★
Plenty of choice at Cala Tarida with a diving school called **Orca Sub Diving Centre**, with English-speaking instructors, at the Club Hotel Tarida Beach. ☎ 971 80 63 07

BEACHES
Cala Tarida is long and sandy with excellent facilities and is very good for children. Cala d'Hort is smaller and can get crowded, but is in a very special location. There are several other more secluded beaches along this coast, some accessible by car, others only by hiring a boat.

EXCURSIONS

You're not too far from either Sant Antoni (see page 30) or Ibiza Town (see page 12), where there is an excellent range of shopping and eating possibilities.

RESTAURANTS

El Carmen €€ Overlooks the middle of the beach, with views out to the island and a typical Spanish menu: fish, *paella*, pizza, meat dishes. ⓐ Cala d'Hort ❶ 971 18 74 49 ❻ Open 12.30–23.30 (Mar–Oct)

C'as Mila €€ Right above the beach, with English-speaking owners who serve up casual lunches and slightly smarter romantic evening meals. Choose your lobster or shellfish from the tanks, or go for the catch of the day. Plenty of meat dishes too. Sometimes there is live music on Saturday night. ⓐ Cala Tarida ❶ 971 80 61 93 ❻ Open 13.00–16.00 and 19.00–midnight

Chiringuito Tarida € ⓐ Right on the beach with a shady terrace and an economical, varied menu. ❻ 09.00–midnight.

Posta del Sol €€ Smart place overlooking the beach, good for *paella* and fresh fish dishes on its charming terrace. ⓐ Cala Tarida ❶ 971 80 63 08 ❻ Open 13.00–17.00 and 19.30–23.30

Restaurante Cala d'Hort €€ Delicious fresh fish, *paella* and crème caramels, with relaxed service. ⓐ Right-hand side of the beach. ❶ 971 18 78 94 ❻ Open noon–23.00 ❶ No credit cards

Stop € This complex is worth a family stop as a change from the beach. There is a children's playground and restaurant with children's menu, plus a bar, pool table, terrace for snacks and a supermarket. ⓐ At the junction of the Cala Tarida and Cala Conta roads ❶ 971 34 69 85 ❻ Open Tues–Sun 13.00–16.30 and 19.30–midnight, Mon 13.00–16.30

○ *A cove at Cala Tarida*

SHOPPING

There are several small supermarkets/souvenir shops along the main street in Cala Tarida, such as the **Supermarket Cala Sol** (good for booze and beach gear), **Supermarket Stop II** and the **Cala Tarida Supermarket**. Half-way down to the beach is another shop that sells beach gear, ice creams, newspapers and so on. In Cala d'Hort, the **Boutique Azibi** is a stylish little shop just a short walk back from the beach selling smart sarongs and a range of beachwear.

Sant Antoni/San Antonio Bay
beaches and boat trips

The area generally referred to as Sant Antoni Bay runs south from the town of Sant Antoni. This is a big bay, and there are plenty of small resorts and beaches in both directions from the main town. The first main area you come to is called Cala de Bou, on the far side of Sant Antoni's harbour which these days is more or less a continuation of the main town. It makes a good base if you don't want to be in the absolute heart of club-land, but able to reach it easily if you want to.

Cala de Bou has several small beaches, so the crowds tend to get dispersed among them. They're all within walking distance if you want a change of scene, though of course the hotels have all the facilities you might want anyway – and remember you don't have to be resident there to enjoy using them.

Further round the Bay is Port des Torrent, an old village that has become a favourite tourist centre. A little further on is the incredibly popular beach of Cala Bassa, in a lovely bay backed by cliffs. From the top of these there's a terrific view back to Sant Antoni, from where regular boat trips bring plenty of day visitors.

If you hire a car to explore the lovely south-west corner of Ibiza, be sure to get a good road map. There are so many twists and turns, so many minor roads and so few signposts, it's very easy to get lost.

SHOPPING

No lack of conventional supermarket/souvenir shops. Well-stocked, especially for British brands, is **Casa Lorenzo supermarket** on Avenida Dr Fleming. It takes credit cards too.

▶ *Sant Antoni Bay*

THINGS TO SEE & DO
Cycling ★
From Cala de Bou to Cala Conta. There is a route from Sant Antoni Bay to the closest beach, Cala Bassa. If you have enough time continue to Cala Conta. Enjoy the landscape and views.

Walking ★★
Take a stroll around the boat-filled bay. The waterfront promenade is lined with cafés, shops and restaurants and there is always plenty of activity. The uninhabited island of Conillera, with its lighthouse, dominates the view. It is possible to take a small boat there and walk among the pine trees and wild flowers.

EXCURSIONS
Climb Sa Talaia ★★
If you're feeling energetic, head south to Sant Josep, from where it's about a two-hour walk to the top of Ibiza's highest peak at 475 m (1560 ft), and back.

Sant Rafel ★★
This village on the road to Ibiza Town has good views of Dalt Vila from the plaza. It is the main spot for ceramic production, so look out for local shops, and village potters. For a treat, dine at L'Éléphant, an up-market restaurant with stylish surroundings. At night there are good views from the outdoor terrace of the illuminated old town. The menu is mostly French and Italian. ❶ 971 19 80 56/971 19 83 54 ❷ Open 20.00–01.00

RESTAURANTS
The bay area is very well off for eating places, whether you want Spanish, British, Indian, Chinese or maybe Tex-Mex.

🍴 **Banyan Palace Thai Restaurant** €€€ New and exquisite Thai restaurant with a sophisticated atmosphere. ⓐ Avenida de San Augustin 73, Cala de Bou ❶ 971 34 77 35

Java €€ Just off the bay road, this family-run restaurant provides a good selection of local and international dishes. Large terrace. ⓐ Carrer Castello 4 ⓣ 971 34 20 27 ⓛ Open 11.00–16.00 and 19.00–03.00

Magon €€ Close to the beach at Port des Torrent, Magon has a covered garden terrace. Steaks, fresh fish and daily specials are the highlights of the menu. ⓐ Port des Torrent ⓣ 971 34 02 98 ⓛ Open 19.00–01.00

Mei Ling II € Popular Chinese restaurant with a lovely dining terrace. All the usual sweet and sour dishes, noodles, crackers, seafood and spare ribs. Families and groups like this place because those who don't want to eat Chinese can order from the pizza/burger menu of the nearby restaurant owned by the same family. ⓐ Look out for the huge pagoda on the main road towards Sant Antoni ⓣ 971 34 43 22 ⓛ Open 13.00–02.00

Sa Soca €€ Just over 1 km (½ mile) south on the road to Sant Josep is this family restaurant serving steaks, *paella*, lamb and stews: a good mix of Spanish and international cooking. ⓣ 971 34 16 20 ⓛ Open 13.00–15.30 and 19.00–midnight, closed Mon

NIGHTLIFE

If you're looking for clubs, then Sant Antoni's the place to go. There are also lots of family bars, many of them with bouncy castles for the children and most with karaoke or other entertainment.

The club **Summum** hosts 'Gold', the 1980s night, every week (ⓐ Carrer Burgos, Edificio Cala Blanca, Sant Antoni Bay ⓣ Club 971 34 39 97; Office 971 34 00 34).

Kumharas is an ideal place for a quiet drink at sunset. You may also find fire-eaters, jugglers and a range of musical performers providing entertainment (ⓐ On the beach, off the main road at Cala de Bou ⓛ Open 20.00 until late).

Sant Antoni/San Antonio
party atmosphere

Ibiza's second town is popular with clubbers. However, the party atmosphere does not start until late in the evening, and there are quieter areas around the town.

It's hard to believe that this was a tiny fishing village about 30 years ago, blessed with a large natural harbour. Tourism came, and the village grew, then the club scene arrived, and the place grew again.

The harbour is one of the town's focal points for an evening stroll or daytime activity, such as booking a boat trip or just sitting on the terrace of one of the many bars and cafés, watching the people and boats go by. At the eastern end in the middle of a roundabout is the 'egg' statue celebrating Christopher Columbus, who possibly came from Ibiza – though several other places claim him too. When he was trying to raise money to find a route through to the Far East, Columbus was told the route was impossible. He took an egg and asked people if they also thought it was impossible to stand the egg upright. When they said that it was, he gently cracked the base to flatten it, and stood it on end. 'Nothing is impossible,' he said. The same might be said of Sant Antoni, especially in the bars, cafés, pubs and clubs in the West End area and out of town.

THINGS TO SEE & DO
Aquarium Cap Blanca ★
This natural cave with its shallow waters was once used by fishermen to protect their catch. Now it's been turned into an illuminated grotto and aquarium showing off the local sea creatures – great for children. There's also a chance to swim outside and have a drink on the bar terrace.
ⓐ Cova de ses Llegostes, Cala Gracio ⓣ 630 73 00 08 ⓦ www.aquarium-capblanca.com ⓛ Open 10.00–21.00 ⓘ Admission charge

◐ *One of Sant Antoni's many clubs*

Glass-bottomed boat trips ★★

There's a choice of several boat trips from the harbour at Sant Antoni. They all offer much the same tour, visiting the bays of Cala Tarida, Cala Vadella and others, and also the island of Es Vedrà, so choose one at the time and price to suit you. It's a good chance to see the marine life in the local waters, and at the same time you'll see something of the island.

Go-karting ★★

There's a track on the edge of town, along the road to Sant Rafel.
ⓣ 971 34 38 05 ⓛ Open 10.00–midnight

Parasailing ★

Fly 200 m (656 ft) over the bay for a bird's-eye view of Sant Antoni and the surrounding area. ⓐ Jimmy at Hotel Es Pins Sailing School and Sant Antoni Harbour ⓣ 606 82 25 02

Promenade by night ★★★

A great way to work up an appetite, whether for food or a night on the town, is to go for a stroll along the promenade. If you're not into clubbing, at least you'll be entertained by watching those who are. At the fountains near the egg statue, there is a light and music show in the evenings.

Sailing and windsurfing ★★

At Arenal Beach, there's a qualified English-speaking instructor at **Vela Náutica** sailing school, where boats, windsurfs and kayaks can be rented.
ⓣ 607 71 89 67

Scenic train trip ★★

Kids and adults will love the two-hour ride on this miniature train which takes you out into the countryside, with a free drink at a terrace bar half-way round. ⓐ Starts at the main roundabout where Avenida Dr Fleming meets the harbour promenade ⓛ Daily departures ⓘ Admission charge.

EXCURSION

Cala Gració ★

At the northern end of Sant Antoni and accessible from there by car or boat, Cala Gració is small, but almost a resort in itself. There is a small beach, and several bars, cafés and restaurants.

Sa Bresca € is a pleasant sunset-watching spot which does a good range of meals and snacks including breakfast. ❷ On the beach ❶ 971 34 14 37 ❸ Open 09.00–20.00.

BEACHES

The beach in the centre is small, but it does have the basic facilities. Unfortunately it's right by the road. You can walk north, and over to the far side of the headland, for another small beach at **Caló des Moro**, or take a bus or ferry to one of the many nearby beaches. Small boats leave from the port of Sant Antoni throughout the day and reach the nearest cove in half an hour. **Cala Bassa** is one of the closest, a small bay backed by pine trees so there's lots of shade. It's a popular place, with water-skis and lilos for hire. There are cafés and restaurants behind the beach. You can also catch a bus from the terminal at the port to most of the beaches.

◗ *The daily ritual of watching the sun go down*

SUNSET BARS (see map opposite)

There are three waterside café-bars at Sant Antoni's harbour where people gather for the daily ritual of watching the sun go down over the sea. All of them play ambient trance music to chill out to, or ease you gently into the night ahead. Later in the evening they act as pre-party places for the larger clubs.

Café del Mar €€ ❶ Once *the* sunset bar to go to, Café del Mar is still a popular spot with a resident DJ, although it doesn't serve food. ❸ Carrer Vara de Rey 27 ❶ 971 34 25 16 ● Open 17.00–01.00

Café Mambo €€ ❷ During the day, this a good place to go for something to eat and to hang out on the beach in front. Later at sunset it fills up with a cocktail-drinking crowd. ❸ Carrer Vara de Rey 40 ❶ 971 34 66 38 ● Open 11.00–04.00

Coastline Café €€ ❸ Upmarket bar restaurant, ideal for pre-club parties, watching the sunset, eating or just relaxing, perhaps in one of the swimming pools. ❸ Carrer de Cervantes 50, Caló des Moro ❶ 971 34 85 53 ❾ www.coastlinecafe.com ● Open noon–01.00

USEFUL INFORMATION
Banks
Found throughout Sant Antoni town and bay, banks are open 08.30–14.00 hours Monday to Friday. Outside of these hours you can use the cashpoint machines which usually accept English bank cards as well as credit cards.

Tourist Information Office
A small hut near the 'egg' has maps, literature about the island and details of activities. ❶ 971 34 01 11 ● Mon–Fri 09.30–20.30, Sat–Sun 09.30–13.30

CALA GRACIO
AQUARIUM CAP BLANCA

CAN GERMA
CALA SALADA

RIBAS 1 FERRER

C. MOSSÈN

C. MENENDEZ

C. DEL MAR

AV. ISIDOR MACABICH

C. DE CATALUNYA

C. D'ALACANT

C. BARCELONA

C. SANTA ROSALIA

C. DE LA SOLEDAT

C. DE CERVANTES

C. DEL PROGRES

C. DE SANT RAFEL

C.D'ANTON RIQUER

RAMON

C. DE RAMON Y CAJAL

FRUIT & VEGETABLE
MARKET

C. GENERAL PRIM

C. DE VARA DE REY

C. DE SANT AGNES

C. AMPLE

C. VELAZQUEZ

C. DE MADRID

C.DE VARA DE REY

BARTMEU VICENT

Sanrafel
West end

CASA
ALFONSO

C. DE SANT ANTONI

MAY SHOPPING
CENTRE

IBIZA

C. DEL GENERAL BALANZAT

THE
"EGG"

DEL FAR

SAN JOSEP
ARENAL BEACH
SANT ANTONI
HARBOUR

0   250   500 m

0   ¼ mile

Port de
Sant Antoni

N

39

To get a sun-lounger or a table at any one of the popular sunset bars, get there at least an hour before sunset. If you don't make it, you can always sit on the sand and soak up the relaxed end-of-day atmosphere.

🔺 *Eating out in Sant Antoni*

RESTAURANTS (see map on page 39)

The Curry Club €€ **❹** Choose from a range of Indian dishes. This is a tranquil place, away from the mayhem of the West End, where you can eat in the beautifully designed restaurant or in its tropical gardens. ⓐ Corner of Carrer Sant Antoni and Madrid ① 971 34 36 04 ⓛ Open 19.00–midnight

Jamel's Bistro €€ **❺** Chicken with stuffing, pork with apple, and pepper steak in delicious sauces are on the menu at this English-style bistro serving French, international and vegetarian dishes. ⓐ Carrer General Prim 14 ① 971 34 01 17 ⓛ Open 19.00–01.00

Mei Ling €€ **❻** A big, popular Chinese restaurant on the main promenade near the fountain. All the usual dishes, like sweet-and-sour pork and spicy prawns, but you can also just order chips and curry sauce. ⓐ Carrer Ample 1 ① 971 34 34 14 ⓛ Open 17.00–midnight, 17.00–01.00 (July and Aug)

Rincón del Pepe €€ **❼** A great *tapas* bar. Also serves steak, schnitzel and Spanish food. ⓐ One block back from the front on Carrer Sant Mateu 6 ① 971 34 06 97 ⓛ Mon–Sat 11.00–01.00, Sun 19.00–01.00

Tijuana €€ **❽** A Mexican and Tex-Mex restaurant where dishes like *burritos* (flour tortillas filled with vegetables or meat and cheese) and barbecue ribs are served with margaritas and Mexican beers in a lively atmosphere. ⓐ Carrer Ramón y Cajal 23 ① 971 34 24 73 ⓛ Sun–Thurs 18.30–01.00, Fri and Sat 18.30–02.00

ALTERNATIVE NAMES
Sant Antoni is also known as San Antonio. In fact, its full name is Sant Antoni de Portmany, but just about everyone calls it plain San An.

SHOPPING

 There are plenty of souvenir shops and supermarkets. Out of curiosity you might try the **Casa Alfonso**, simply because it was the first supermarket on Ibiza. It stocks local and British foods and has an off-licence (ⓐ Near the junction of Carrer Ample and Sant Antoni (Carrer Progrès 8) ☎ 971 34 05 10 ⏰ Mon–Sat 09.00–22.30, closed Sun).

Further along Carrer Sant Antoni is the **May Shopping Centre** on five floors: sports goods, clothes, souvenirs galore, brand names, booze and cigarettes (ⓐ Carrer de Sant Antoni 13 ☎ 971 34 00 86 ⏰ Mon–Sat 09.30–22.00, Sun 10.00–14.00 and 17.00–21.00).

There's a fruit and fish market open every morning until 14.00. Ask for *el mercado*.

NIGHTLIFE

The West End is filled with drinking places and geared towards young clubbers. Most of the bars and pubs stay open until the early hours. Some of the more popular places include **Murphy's Irish Pub**, **Koppas**, **Joe Spoons** and **Cheers**.

The Ship Inn is an English pub with pints and darts and an authentic atmosphere (ⓐ Carrer Bartolome Vicente Ramon, West End ⏰ Open noon–02.00).

Simple Art Club is a popular place with a big dance floor and flaming tequilas (ⓐ On the main West End drag ⏰ Open until 06.00 hours).

Play 2 and **Nightlife** are two other spots in the West End where you can drink and dance the night away until the early hours. See pages 68–75 for more information in Ibiza's club scene and evening entertainment options.

🔵 *Sant Antoni comes alive as the sun fades*

Portinatx & Sant Miquel
charming northern bays

**These two resorts on the rugged north-west coast of Ibiza are very
different. Sant Miquel is a small place built up around a lovely bay
of a beach, and is more correctly known as Port de Sant Miquel. The
main town of Sant Miquel is a short way inland, and is hardly affected
by tourism, though it does offer a wider range of shopping than the
supermarkets and souvenir shops. By contrast, Portinatx (pronounced
'port-ee-natch') is a pretty family resort, the main resort on this coast.
It has several beaches, lovely clear waters and lots of eating places and
bars. There are cliffs all around and some good walks if you fancy
getting some exercise.**

THINGS TO SEE & DO
Can Marça Caves ★★★
Take the cliff road west of Sant Miquel to these illuminated limestone
caves. ❶ 971 33 47 76 ❷ Open 10.30–18.30 ❸ Admission charge

Dancing in Sant Miquel village ★★
There is a traditional dancing display outside the church in this inland
village every Thursday at about 18.00. There's also a craft market on
Thursdays 18.00–22.00. There is a special bus service to Sant Miquel
from Ibiza Town at 17.00.

Water sports ★★
Try snorkelling at Portinatx, or learn scuba diving at **Sant Miquel
Diving Centre** (❶ 971 33 45 39 ❿ www.divingcenter-sanmiguel.com).
Windsurfing, boats and pedalos are available at both beaches.
You can also try water-skiing at Sant Miquel.

◀ *Portinatx has clear waters and quiet coves as well as water sports and walks*

EXCURSIONS

Take a boat trip from either resort to one of the quieter bays along the coast. Keen walkers might like to tackle the old bridle-path, which is 11 km (7 miles) long and leads to the inland village of Sant Joan. Take plenty of water with you to drink along the way, and do not attempt the walk in the full heat of the day – some parts are very steep.

BEACHES

Portinatx has three main beaches of which the quietest is the last one you come to at the end of the road. There are fishing boats lined up on the shore and it is a good place to watch the sunset. There are also some quiet coves, such as **Cala Xarraca** and **S'illot**, which can also be reached by boat.

Sant Miquel has one main beach which is always busy, but if you want somewhere quieter and you have a car, drive north-east to nearby **Cala de Benirràs**.

RESTAURANTS & BARS

All the following are in Portinatx, unless otherwise stated.

C'as Mallorqui €€ One of the most popular eating places with its large terrace overlooking the beach and harbour, plus good food, including fresh fish, *paella* and authentic local cooking. Access by steep steps. ❶ 971 32 05 05 Ⓦ www.casmallorqui.com Ⓛ Open 09.00–23.00

Delboy's English Bar € Hard to miss, with the yellow Reliant Robin parked outside. Roast beef and other English food and evening entertainment from live sports coverage to karaoke and hypnotism. ❸ Next to the coach park at the main beach ❶ 971 32 05 46 Ⓛ Open 10.00–late

El Puerto € Serves soups, meat dishes, pizza, fresh fish, lobster and *paella*. ❸ Right on the small beach, accessed by steps ❶ 971 32 07 56 Ⓛ Open noon–16.00 and 19.00–23.00

Port Balansat €€ Some say this is the best fish shop on the island, with local specialities such as *paella*, fish stew, fish soup, squid fried in batter and pizza. ❸ In Sant Miquel, to the left of the beach as you approach it ❶ 971 33 45 27 ❷ Open 13.00–16.30 and 19.00–23.30

Restaurante Jardín del Mar €€ Complete with a mini-golf course. Choose from pizza, fresh fish and great salads. ❸ In a prime spot overlooking the main beach ❶ 971 32 07 52 ❷ Open 10.00–16.00 and 18.30–midnight

Restaurant Real € Serves the usual meat and fish, plus spaghetti, pizza and lobster. It also serves afternoon teas with strawberries and cream. Good value for money. ❸ Up in the village ❶ 971 32 05 61 ❷ Open for breakfast 09.00–noon, lunch noon–17.00, dinner 19.00–23.00

Sant Miquel € A pizzeria serving a full range of restaurant meals. ❸ Sant Miquel ❶ 971 33 48 67 ❷ Open 10.00–16.30 and 19.00–midnight, closed Wed

Vicente's Bar € An English bar with live sports coverage and live acts. ❸ Near Delboy's ❷ Open 20.00–03.00

SHOPPING

The beach resort of Sant Miquel has the usual row of souvenir and beach shops; all the 'real' shops are found in the inland village of Sant Miquel. Portinatx has a good little cluster of bars, restaurants and shops in the town itself. For a good choice of drinks there's the **Boozy Buys** off-licence and money exchange, which sells some of the cheapest alcohol on the island, and further up there are a couple of clothes shops. On the opposite side of the road from these, in another row of shops, you'll find **Rincón Verde**, which has a wide range of ceramics and paintings.

Cala Sant Vicent
palm-fringed bay

As you approach the resort of Cala Sant Vicent along twisting hill roads, you will see some of the pine forests which caused the Greeks to call Ibiza and Formentera 'the Pine Islands'. Cala Sant Vicent is a tiny place but well worth a day out because it has a great beach with lots of facilities, and there are plenty of excellent eating places overlooking the beach. Some of the freshest fish on the island is served here.

A few years ago there was nothing here except for the pretty inlet with a long and gently curving sandy beach. However, a string of small hotels has been developed behind the little promenade, and there are also enough shops and cheaper eating places here now to satisfy most visitors. The promenade is fringed with palm trees and is traffic-free, which means, with the shallow waters, this is an especially good place to take children.

There's very little to do at Cala Sant Vicent other than eat and enjoy the beach, but it does have water sports, volleyball and even a mini-golf course. There are some good walks, too, for the more energetically minded. You may come across **Sant Vicent Church** and traditional old farmhouses dotted about the hillsides on your travels.

THINGS TO SEE & DO
Water sports ★
Pedalos and boats can be hired, and there is a diving school, **Mundo Azul** (☏ 971 32 03 05/mobile: 637 75 91 40 ⓦ www.mundoazulibiza.com).

If you are heading off on a walk, always let someone know where you're going and when you hope to be back, especially if going alone. It's very easy to twist an ankle on rough rural tracks.

◗ *The bay at Cala Sant Vicent*

EXCURSIONS

Es Cuieram ★

Walk to the cave of Es Cuieram, an important archaeological find on Ibiza. It was once a shrine to Tanit, the Carthaginian goddess, and when it was rediscovered in 1907, it was full of gold medallions and terracotta figures. Many of the finds are on display in the Museu Arqueològic de Dalt Vila (see page 18), so there's not much to see in the cave now. There are occasional guided tours from Sant Vicent village which the tourist office should be able to give you details on.
🕐 Open 24 hours a day ❶ Admission free

Punta Grossa ★

Walk north to the cliffs of Punta Grossa, with wonderful views back to Cala Sant Vicent and along the coast to the north. Take care when walking as the cliffs are steep and unprotected.

Sant Carles ★★

If you've got a hired car take the road towards Santa Eulària and make a stop in the pretty little inland village of Sant Carles (see page 78). You'll understand why the hippies of the 1960s made it one of their main bases on Ibiza.

Tagomago ★★

Take a boat to the private offshore island of Tagomago, which is to the south of Cala Sant Vicent. This is a good place for a picnic and it has two tiny beaches. It's better suited for swimming and fishing though than sunbathing.

BEACHES

The beach at Sant Vicent is in a beautiful cove and is very well maintained with excellent facilities. There are other good beaches you can get to by boat or by road, at **Es Figueral** and **Pou des Lleó** to the south. The beach at Es Figueral is narrow and sandy and has good water sports facilities and beach amenities.

If you like to strip off on the beach you might be tempted by the fact that Ibiza's second official nudist beach (the other is at **Es Cavallet**) is south of here at **Aiguës Blanques**. It's only a narrow stretch of sand, though, and is far from being the best beach on the island. You'd be better advised to try and find yourself a private secluded cove.

RESTAURANTS

 Can Gat €€ The original 'fish house' of Cala San Vicent. ⓐ On the beach ⓣ 971 32 01 23 ⓒ Open 11.00–22.00

Can Miguel des Port €€ Especially good for fish, the speciality being mixed grilled fish. Tuna, squid, mullet and whatever else is in season and freshly landed is also on offer. ⓐ Along the front ⓣ 971 32 00 67 ⓒ Open 13.00–16.00 and 20.00–23.00

 Es Caló €€ An upmarket restaurant serving speciality local fish dishes. ⓐ Right on the seafront ⓣ 971 32 01 40 ⓒ Open 10.00–midnight

 Es Gorch £ Serves both meals and drinks, including cocktails and, during the day, its own fresh orange 'vitamin drink'. ⓐ At the back of the beach, to the right as you approach it ⓣ 971 32 01 44 ⓒ Open 10.30–19.00, closed Mon

SHOPPING

Xaloc, along the front, is a very well-stocked souvenir and general shop, with lots of newspapers and magazines, and a wide range of paperbacks, guidebooks, maps and postcards. For food and other provisions, there's a **Spar** supermarket on the left as you enter Cala Sant Vicent, behind the row of beachfront hotels and opposite Jimmy's Burgers.

Es Canar
bustling modern resort

It wasn't so long ago that there was nothing at Es Canar but a lovely beach. Then, in 1964, enterprising British owners built the Panorama Hotel, and a resort was born. It has developed as much more of a family resort than some others, because of the lovely safe beach and the fact that it's a fair way from the nightlife in Ibiza Town and Sant Antoni.

The fact that Es Canar is quiet does not mean there's nothing to do. There are plenty of bars and restaurants; even on a fortnight's visit you could eat and drink somewhere different every night. There are a handful of English pubs, most with entertainment, and plenty of shops. Although there are no banks here, the resort does have several cashpoint machines.

THINGS TO SEE & DO
Cycling ★
There are two cycle-hire shops in town. Why not spend a day exploring the pretty scenery in the north of the island? The land around here is pretty flat, making it ideal for cyclists. Try **Bicis Kandani** ☎ 971 33 92 64 ⓦ www.kandani.com ⏱ Open Mon–Fri 09.00–13.30 and 16.30–21.00, Sat 09.00–13.30

Glass-bottomed boat trips ★★
Take a look at the creatures that live under the sea, and at a shipwreck off the coast of Es Canar, in one of the regular tours from the harbour.

The Hippy Market ★★★
Held every Wednesday at Punta Arabi from about 09.00 until 19.00. Follow the signs from Es Canar and it's just a short walk to the many dozens of stalls selling clothes, jewellery, paintings, carvings and leather.

◄ *The busy beach at Es Canar*

There's a self-service restaurant in the centre of the market, and all sorts of performers ready to provide some impromptu entertainment. There's also a day nursery and information office. ❶ 971 33 06 50
Ⓦ www.hippymarket.com

Watch your wallets and purses at the Hippy Market. Theft is not a major problem, but it is a favourite place for pickpockets due to the jostling crowds, especially at the height of the season.

Water sports ★★
Try water sports at **Cesar's Water Sports** in S'Argamassa. The windsurfing and sailing school has parascending, boat hire and lots of other facilities.
❶ 971 33 09 19/670 62 99 61 Ⓔ cesarjerez@ctv.es

BEACHES
Es Canar has a lovely crescent-shaped sandy beach with lots of facilities and restaurants, which is why it's so popular with families. A short walk away is the quieter – and just as attractive but smaller – **Cala Nova**, located near the campsite. There's also a nice beach at **S'Argamassa**, backed by pine trees and with all the basic amenities, plus pedalos for hire, and a handy restaurant.

SHOPPING
There is a wide selection of shops in the resort. The **Groch** perfume shop is on your right as you enter Es Canar, with a huge stock of well-known names, and jewellery too. **Juma** has a good range of Lladró and Majorica pearls, and also sells crystal, watches and other more expensive items. It's on your right on the street that leaves Es Canar towards Punta Arabi. Don't miss the **Hippy Market** on Wednesdays (see page 53).

EXCURSIONS

From Es Canar you can walk the 6 km (4 miles) south along the coast all the way to Santa Eulària, by heading towards Punta Arabi and then continuing. You'll see coves and quiet beaches, and there are plenty of places to stop for a drink and a rest. You can always get the bus or a taxi back if you're feeling tired. An hour's walk in the other direction leads to Cala Llenya, through pinewoods to another sandy beach.

 Lobster is widely available

 If you're feeling less energetic, take one of the regular boats to nearby beaches or Santa Eulària.

RESTAURANTS & BARS

Las Arenas €€ Next to the bakery/pâtisserie in Es Canar, near the ferry terminus. Has a varied menu ranging from hamburgers and chicken to fresh fish and *paella*. ☎ 971 33 07 90 🕒 Open 08.30–midnight

Bora Bora € At Playa Niu Blau, this well-situated bar and restaurant does everything from snacks to international food, and prides itself on its fresh fish dishes. ☎ 971 33 97 72 🕒 Open 10.30–midnight

Charly's € Situated on the harbour, this is a popular bar and restaurant with live music most nights. 🕒 Open 18.00–04.00

Grannies € This English pub in the centre of Es Canar has a good atmosphere and special drinks offers. 🕒 Open noon–02.00

◆ Es Canar harbour

Jacaranda €€ A great place for breakfasts, snacks, teas, ice creams and cocktails, and also to watch the sunset from the beautiful terrace. ⓐ By the beach in Es Canar, near the ferry terminus ⏰ Open 09.00–02.00

Marbella € The kind of relaxed place where you can have anything from a quick can of Coke to a seafood *paella*, with good service. ⓐ Right on the beach in Es Canar ☎ 971 33 03 65 ⏰ Open 09.30–23.30

New Wave €€ Hidden away in Es Canar, this place has three bars, indoor and outdoor dining, a video room, music and a menu of simple but substantial grub such as steak, chicken, jacket potatoes and salads. ⓐ Can Soldat ☎ 971 33 27 78 ⏰ Open 21.00–06.00

Pizzeria Vivaldi €€ Has a great choice of home-made pizza and other Italian dishes, plus grilled local fish. There's a children's menu too. Regulars get a glass of liqueur from the owner, while children are offered a sweet at the end of the meal. ⓐ In Es Canar, on the right heading towards Punta Arabi ☎ 971 31 90 96 ⏰ Open noon–15.30 and 19.00–midnight

Zodiac € This place, with its own pool and beach, does simple snacks as well as full meals like steak and spaghetti, a great choice of puddings, and there is entertainment later in the evening. ⓐ On the left of the road that leads to Punta Arabi, near the ferry terminus. ☎ 971 33 08 22 ⏰ Open 09.00–16.00 and 18.00–23.00

NIGHTLIFE

Popeye's pub-club has nightly live entertainment, darts, pool and a British menu (ⓐ On the road from Es Canar to the Miami Hotel and Calanova Playa). Just below Popeye's is a disco. There are plenty of other pubs, including the recently renovated **Do Drop Inn** (☎ 660 77 68 55 ⏰ Open noon–01.00, Wed 18.00–01.00), with karaoke, coverage of sports and weekly cinema sessions .

Cala Llonga
the long cove

The small resort of Cala Llonga is popular with families and couples. The pine-backed cove has shallow, safe water, which is great for children. Small ferries run between the beach here and Santa Eulària, which is also reached by bus.

Ideally situated on the east coast between the interesting centres of Santa Eulària and Ibiza Town, Cala Llonga makes a good starting point for day excursions. It is a relaxed place, but there is a good range of shops and restaurants to choose from.

THINGS TO SEE & DO
Riding ★★
Beginners and experienced riders can take a short trip or a half-day ride into the surrounding countryside. Try **Easy Rider** ⓐ Camino d'en Serra ❶ 971 19 65 11

Walking ★★
You can walk over the mountains to Santa Eulària, about two hours away. It's incredibly scenic with great views. As a designated 'Falcon Route' (see Sports & activities, page 103) it is clearly signposted. Either take a taxi back or return along the more inland path for a change of scenery. Make sure you take lots of water with you, cover your head, and don't set off in the heat of the day.

Water sports ★★
Pedalos are available for hire on the beach. **Rumbo Azul Dive Centre** offers PADI courses and daily outings for certified divers (❶ 971 19 66 25 ⓦ www.rumboazul.com).

◀ *The cove at Cala Llonga*

SHOPPING

There are small supermarkets, newsagents and off-licences on the road behind the beach. Every Thursday evening there is a **hippy market** in Cala Llonga that fills the small streets and sells everything from jewellery to clothes and souvenirs. It is open from 18.00 to 23.00 hours. Santa Eulària, with all its speciality shops and hippy stalls, is only ten minutes away by taxi. Similarly, Ibiza Town is a 20-minute ride away.

BEACHES

The main beach is sheltered with fine sand and shallow water which only reaches a depth of a metre (3 ft) when 25 m (30 yd) from the shore.

 Tucked away about 700 m (765 yd) to the south is the small pebble beach of **Sol d'en Serra**. It's a peaceful spot away from the crowds of the main beach.

RESTAURANTS

La Cantina Pub € Serves traditional Sunday lunch, steak and onion and English pies. There is a cocktail list and family games.
ⓐ Just behind the main beach ❶ 971 19 65 88 ❷ Open noon–15.00 and 19.00–midnight, Wed 19.00–midnight

Restaurant Cala Llonga € Choose from fresh fish, shellfish, good meat dishes or just a snack at this restaurant which has sports TV.
ⓐ On the left of the beach ❶ 971 19 64 74 ❷ 09.30–16.00 and 19.00–23.30

Sol d'en Serra Restaurant €€ This restaurant is built on three levels with a terrace and sun-loungers. A full menu is on offer as well as drinks and snacks. ⓐ Overlooking the small beach, at the top of the slope ❶ 971 19 61 76 ❷ Open 10.00–17.00 and 20.00–01.00

🍴 **Wild Asparagus** €€ An up-market poolside restaurant serving steaks, curries and international cuisine. There are also speciality nights. ⓐ Behind the beach ☎ 971 33 15 67 🕐 Open 19.00–23.00, Sun 13.00–15.30, closed Mon

NIGHTLIFE

Cala Llonga is a quiet resort and not really the place for nightlife. There are a few bars, though. **Up 'n' Inn** has karaoke on certain nights of the week. **The Bunch of Grapes** in the Asparagus complex is an English-style pub. There is also a children's funfair in summer.

🔺 *The beach at Cala Llonga*

Santa Eulària/Santa Eulalía
something for everyone

Santa Eulària – also known as Santa Eulalía – is many people's favourite place on Ibiza. It has managed to retain its island identity and local culture while also embracing the visitors who come here for a summer holiday. Its long, curving beach, and the traffic-free promenade behind it, are backed by a string of restaurants, shops, hotels, bars and cafés.

Santa Eulària is the third largest town on Ibiza, after the capital and Sant Antoni, and so the streets beyond the promenade are also filled with shops, bars and cafés, pleasant squares where local people sit in the evening or enjoy a stroll, and some of the best eating places on the island. In short, it seems to have something for everyone.

The main street, Carrer Sant Jaume, is lined with trees and is a good place to wander. Behind, Carrer Sant Vicent is known as the 'street of restaurants' because of its variety of eating places. **Plaza España** is a pleasant spot to sit and watch the world go by as it's filled with flowers, fountains, street-sellers and painters.

 Take an evening walk like the locals do, and sit in one of the cafés to enjoy an early-evening drink as the sun goes down.

THINGS TO SEE & DO
The Ethnological Museum ★
There aren't many museums on Ibiza, so make the most of them. This tiny example traces the town's history and has traditional costumes and jewellery on display, as well as farming implements and musical instruments. ❸ Can Ros, just below the church, Puig de Missa ❶ 971 33 28 45 ❷ meef@cief.es ❸ Mon–Sat 10.00–14.00 and 17.30–20.00, Sun 11.00–13.30

◀ *Santa Eulària promenade*

Galleries ★★

Wander around the town and visit one of its many galleries. As one of the first places on the island to attract foreign residents, it is something of an artistic colony. Some of the galleries and shops have works by internationally exhibited artists.

Marina ★★

The town has an impressive marina. Many of the big yachts here belong to the many foreign residents who have made Santa Eulària their home.

Puig de Missa ★★★

Follow the signs to this hill above the town. It's only about 90 m (295 ft) high but has great views because the land around is mostly quite flat. At the top is the 16th-century church dedicated to Santa Eulària.

The Roman Bridge ★

As you drive in from Ibiza Town you see this recently renovated bridge, built by the Romans in AD 70. Little on the island has survived from those days.

Water sports ★★

Club Náutico de Santa Eulària in the port is a sailing club. ❶ 971 33 11 73

EXCURSIONS
Boat trips ★★

Small ferries run throughout the day between the harbour at Santa Eulària to Ibiza Town, Cala Llonga, Es Canar and the island of Formentera.

Miniature train ★

Take a ride into the countryside on the miniature train that tootles through the town and takes in the Ethnological Museum. The journey lasts almost two hours and includes a free drink at a refreshment stop half-way round. ❸ Leaves from town hall ❶ 971 33 97 72

◐ *Whitewashed buildings in Santa Eulària*

RESTAURANTS

There are three main restaurant areas, one along the promenade, the others along Carrer Sant Vicent and at the yacht marina, which are closed to motor traffic at night.

Ca Na Ribes €€ Has entrances on Sant Vicent and the main street, San Jaume. It has a wide menu including local dishes and international food. Try an Ibizan speciality, like skate in an almond sauce, or just settle for a steak. Courtyard garden inside and ice-cream parlour next door. ❸ Carrer Sant Vicent 44 ❶ 971 33 00 06 ❻ Open 13.00–15.00 and 19.00–23.30, closed Wed

Celler C'an Pere €€ Claims to be Ibiza's oldest restaurant, situated between Carrer Sant Vicent and Carrer San Jaume. Family-owned and offers both local specialities and regular fare. Good seafood too. Choose lobster fresh from the tank. ❸ Carrer Sant Jaume 63 ❶ 971 33 00 56 ❻ Open 12.30–15.30 and 19.00–23.00, until midnight (Aug)

Daffers € Renowned for its excellent cooking and value-for-money, fixed-price, three-course meals, with plenty of choice. French chef and English-speaking staff. ❸ Calle Sant Vicent 57 ❶ 971 33 67 09 ❻ Open Mon–Sat 18.00–23.30 ❶ It is advisable to go early

Sa Llesca €€ Terrace and chill-out area. Specialities include fresh salads, pâté, cold meats and a variety of cheeses. ❸ Santa Eulària Marina, look for a stone tower ❶ 971 33 62 28 ❻ Open 18.00–03.00, closed Mon

Ibiza's club scene

The island has one of the best club scenes in the world. The venues, massive capacity places where thousands have been spent on the interiors, are not equalled even in London. England's best DJs are brought to the island throughout the season. The result is high-quality music in beautiful venues with crowds that always seem to want more. While some clubs cater mainly for British tourists, the larger venues such as Privilege, El Divino and Pacha draw more of a European crowd.

⬥ *Entertaining the crowd at Ibiza's legendary Pacha*

PROMOTERS

It is the promoters and their DJs that make a night, not the venue. The most popular places normally have one big night of the week, which changes from season to season. Check posters, flyers and any of the free magazines that can easily be found at many shops at the port of Ibiza.

COST

Entrance to clubs is expensive. Entry often includes a drink, and you will want to take advantage of this as even the price of a bottle of water is exorbitant in some places. If you buy your ticket in advance you will normally make a saving of about one-sixth, but make sure you buy it from a recognized bar or stand.

Ask your holiday rep about the entertainment packages available. They can get you discounted entrance to certain clubs, free and discounted drinks, and pre-club entertainment most nights of the week.

THE BALEARIC SOUND

The Balearic Sound, known the world over, came out of Ibiza and its sister islands in the Balearics, after house music first took off in England. Club-goers picked up on the music, which combined house with the more rhythmic sound of flamenco and Spanish folk music. You'll hear it almost everywhere you go, and particularly at the sunset bars.

Many promoters at the big clubs on the road to Ibiza Town will refund the cost of a taxi there for three or more people. Look out for details on promotional literature and tickets.

OPENING TIMES

Most clubs open their doors around midnight, really get going at about 02.00 hours and don't close until 06.00 or 07.00 hours. Many of the big nights have pre-parties where people meet to have a few drinks and get in the mood. Check on promotional literature and tickets. **Space** at Platja d'en Bossa is the after-party club, opening all day from 07.00.

VENUES

Amnesia ⓐ Sant Rafel, on the road between Ibiza Town and Sant Antoni
ⓣ 971 79 80 41 ⓦ www.amnesia.es

El Divino ⓐ Ibiza Nueva Harbour, Ibiza Town
ⓣ 971 19 01 76/971 31 83 38 ⓦ www.eldivino-ibiza.com

Eden ⓐ Avenida Dr Fleming, Sant Antoni ⓣ 971 34 25 51
ⓦ www.edenibiza.com

Pacha ⓐ Avenida 8 Agost, Ibiza Town ⓣ 971 31 36 00
ⓦ www.pacha.com

Es Paradis Terrenal ⓐ Avenida Dr Fleming, Sant Antoni ⓣ 971 34 66 00
ⓦ www.esparadis.com

Privilege ⓐ Sant Rafel, on the road between Ibiza Town and Sant Antoni
ⓣ 971 19 80 86 ⓦ www.privilegeibiza.com

Space ⓐ Platja d'en Bossa ⓣ 971 39 67 93 ⓦ www.space-ibiza.com

FOAM PARTIES

Foam and water parties are a bit of an Ibiza institution, although not as popular as they once were. The foam or water is released from the ceiling to soak the people on the dance floor, whose reaction can be anything from skidding to stripping. The dance floor at **Es Paradis** actually fills with water and becomes a swimming pool. Es Paradis in Sant Antoni has a 'Water Festival' twice a week in summer. **Amnesia** at Sant Rafel holds a twice-weekly foam party, while **Privilege**, also in Sant Rafel, holds a weekly foam session.

THE DISCO BUS

Calling at the main nightclubs and hotels, the service runs from **Sant Antoni** (Passeig de la Mar) to **Ibiza Town** (Avenida Isidoro Macabich), stopping at **Port des Torrent**, **Platja d'en Bossa**, **Santa Eulària**, **Es Canar** and **Cap Martinet** on six linked routes. It is a cheap alternative to taxis, which can be difficult to find in summer. Check times on the website ⓦ www.ibizabus.com

◗ *Eden disco*

Evening entertainment

Many tour companies offer a package of events that changes weekly or fortnightly. Some nights are arranged to give you a range of pre-club entertainment, with discounted entry and free drinks in bars and clubs. Other events are designed to keep the whole family entertained and are suitable for children. Here are some of the typical tours on offer.

Foam Party ★★★
Amnesia is Ibiza's club home of foam parties (see page 70). Every Sunday and Wednesday a huge jet of foam covers the dance floor with bubbles.
ⓐ On the road between Ibiza Town and Sant Antoni **ⓦ** www.amnesia.es

Fun Fair ★★
Fun fair with amusements, dodgems, bungee rides and much more entertainment for all the family. **ⓐ** On the Avenida Dr Fleming, close to Es Paradis

Summum ★★
At the **Summum Club** in Sant Antoni Bay you can listen to an alternative to house – anything from jazz to flamenco. Summum is an up-market venue, one of the very first clubs to be established on the island.
ⓐ Carrer Burgos, Edificio Cala Blanca, Sant Antoni Bay **ⓣ** 971 34 00 34 (office)/971 34 39 97 (club)

Kiwi Fiesta – Hangi Night ★★
A different way to spend the night with the whole family together. Every Thursday in an old *finca*, try a Maori recipe. Special Kiddies Club.
ⓐ Can Truy, Santa Eulària **ⓣ** 971 32 50 73 **ⓔ** cantruy@terra.es

---

ⓐ *Ibiza offers an extensive range of evening entertainment*

Murphy's Night ★

Enjoy a night out, Irish-style. You will be served dinner and drinks in an authentic Irish pub where there is draught Guinness, Irish whiskey and lots of fun. Suitable for all the family, this event includes a cabaret, competitions and a live band. ⓐ Murphy's Irish Bar, Platja d'en Bossa

OTHER NIGHTLIFE AREAS

Ibiza Town and Sant Antoni are, without doubt, the two places which contain the biggest concentration of nightlife, ranging from the avant-garde, where you can hear and dance to the latest music, to the pleasant terraces and bars of the leisure marinas and fishing ports. It must be said, however, that the nightlife is not just confined to the setting of the Ibizan capital's port. Every holiday resort has its own entertainment for all tastes.

Sant Antoni ★

On the harbour promenade, fountains dance as music is played, every night at about 21.00.

Es Paradis ★★

Like no club you've seen before. This huge venue has different floors with marble columns and giant plants that reach up to the glass pyramid roof, which can be opened to the elements. There are several bars, pool tables, a central dancing podium and special 'water parties' on Wednesdays and Saturdays. ⓐ Avenida Dr Fleming, Sant Antoni ⓣ 971 34 66 00 ⓦ www.esparadis.com

> ↘ Different events are arranged for almost every night of the week so you've always got something to do. Check the details with your holiday rep.

● *Enjoy a quiet drink while watching the glorious sunsets*

🔺 *Sant Miquel*

Around the island

Ibiza is very small and hiring a car for a few days will enable you to see most of it. There are small coves for beach lovers to discover, and some of the inland villages are beautiful. The following suggested route takes in many of the best places – and while exploring, you might find a resort for your next holiday on Ibiza.

Don't book a car too early in your holiday. Wait until you've seen what days the various optional excursions are on. You can usually negotiate a better rate if you want the vehicle for more than one day.

THE ROUTE

This circular route starts and ends in Ibiza Town, although of course you can join it anywhere you like. Depending on how long you stop at each point, this route could take a whole day.

Jésus

On leaving Ibiza Town (see page 12) take the road marked Santa Eulària. As you leave the town behind, watch for the right turning to Jesús – a name that's hard to miss. In fact you might like to stop in this tiny hamlet and visit its church, **Nostra Mare de Jésus** (❸ Open 09.30–12.30 and 16.30–19.00). Inside is a painting of the Virgin and Child, thought to date from the 16th century and regarded as the greatest work of art on the island. It is an unusual depiction of Mary breastfeeding the baby Jesus.

Cala Llonga

On leaving Jesús head for Cala Llonga (see page 59), a lovely beach. Take a break at the beach or continue on to rejoin the main road heading for Santa Eulària. As you approach the town look on your left for the hill of Puig de Missa, topped by a white church. On your right, as you cross the only river in the Balearic Islands (it's usually dried up), look out for the old Roman bridge.

Santa Eulària

Santa Eulària (see page 63) is well worth a long stop, then afterwards carry on to **Es Canar** (see page 53), a smaller resort that's still quite lively. Use the ring road on Wednesday mornings, unless you can be very early, as the weekly hippy market attracts traffic from all over Ibiza.

Sant Carles

Leave Es Canar by the way you came in, and take the right-hand turn where the main road turns sharp left. This leads through some lovely scenery to the attractive little village of Sant Carles, a popular hippy haunt in the 1960s. There is an interesting hippy market here at **Las Dalias** on Saturdays and on Monday nights. Beyond here the road winds through pine-covered hills and down to the tiny resort of **Cala Sant Vicent** (see page 48), with a nice beach.

Portinatx

Head back uphill and take the road to **Sant Joan**, another pleasant town. Beyond here take a right turn down to the much busier holiday resort of Portinatx (see page 45), a good spot for lunch – the **Ca's Mallorqui** restaurant is well recommended (see page 46).

Balafia

Take the road back towards Ibiza Town and, just beyond the turning to Sant Joan, you have a decision to make. If you're a nervous driver, take the first right turn to **Sant Miquel**. If you fancy a bit of adventure, carry on and watch carefully for the right turn to **Balafia**, almost opposite the turning to Es Canar. Bump along the rough track to Balafia. Its Moorish heritage, ancient buildings and fortified towers make it one of the most unusual inland villages. Carry on through it and pick up the better road to **Santa Gertrudis**. This pretty village is an ideal place to stop and have a drink and some olives at one of the pavement cafés.

Sant Antoni/San Antonio

After a visit to the caves of **Port de Sant Miquel**, return to the town of
Sant Miquel and turn right to Sant Antoni (see page 30).

Cala d'Hort

Leave Sant Antoni on the Sant Josep road, but before you reach the town
itself look for the right turn to Cala d'Hort (see page 26). This little bay
is well worth the detour, with its view of the offshore island of **Es Vedrà**.
When you leave you can either retrace your route or take a right turn
marked **Sant Josep**, an interesting little village worth a visit. Both routes
are similar in distance, and take you back to the main road where you
turn right to head back into Ibiza Town.

● *The Ca's Mallorqui restaurant in Portinatx*

RESTAURANTS & BARS

Ama Lur €€€ Winner of the Best Restaurant of the Island award in 2001 and 2002. Excellent service and a good selection of wines. ⓐ 2.3 km (1.4 miles) on the road from Ibiza Town to Santa Gertrudis ① 971 31 45 54 ① Open 20.00–midnight

Bon Lloc €€ This bar and restaurant is a pleasant place to stop for a drink, snack or meal. ⓐ Jesús, on the main road running through the village ① 971 31 18 13 ① Open 07.00–01.00 (bar), 20.00–midnight (restaurant)

 Peralta € Good, filling Ibizan dishes are served alongside international cuisine throughout the day. ⓐ Sant Carles ① 971 33 98 94 ① Open 11.00–midnight

Santa Gertrudis € Has several bars which serve delicious sandwiches and *tapas*. ⓐ Santa Gertrudis

Island Tour ★★★

Take in the island's varied highlights in a tailor-made tour that has something for everyone. You could watch potters and shop at a ceramic factory, visit a distillery to try as you buy, and explore beautiful Dalt Vila (see page 18) and the shops at the heart of Ibiza Town. There are also opportunities to take photos at the dramatic island of Es Vedrà and the unusual landscape of the saltflats. This is a relaxed way to get to know the island and as such a whole day is required. If you want to see everything in more depth, however, divide the island in two – one half one day, the other half the next. Visit the local tourist office or ask your holiday representative to find out about tour operators.

◗ *The bay of Cala d'Hort*

Cruises ★★★

Sail along the coast of Ibiza and enjoy secluded coves from the comfort of a boat. The glass-bottomed boats allow you to see brightly coloured fish and other underwater creatures. These cruises tend to last a full day, with drinks served on board and lunch at a beach where you can also swim. Some companies offer themed cruises such as a pirate trip, complete with a treasure hunt on the beach. Find out more information from the local tourist office or your holiday representative.

DRIVING TIPS

Spanish drivers have a reckless reputation, but those on Ibiza are generally safer and you should have few problems. The main hazards include:

- Local drivers taking corners in the middle of the road – keep well over to the right yourself when taking a bend.
- Steep winding ascents and descents – make full use of the gears.
- Other tourists, who may not be used to driving abroad.
- Drivers not using indicators.

◀ *Ibiza Town, overlooking the marina*

Formentera
Ibiza's island neighbour

Ibiza's nearest neighbour in the Balearic Islands is a short, but some-times choppy, hop away. It takes just over an hour on the conventional ferries, and half an hour on the faster catamaran service – and the fares vary. Ferries run from 07.30–20.30 almost every hour. In high season the frequency increases. The boats go from the western end of the harbour in Ibiza Town, and you buy your tickets in advance inside the building there (Estación Maritima).

Formentera is a world away from Ibiza. There is tourism here but on a much smaller scale, and the island has a more peaceful atmosphere, with its wonderful stretches of white sandy beach. The island is very rural, with a scattering of small villages and a population of only 7500 people – compared to 35,000 in Ibiza Town alone.

The island is flatter and less wooded than Ibiza, but there is one dramatic height – **La Mola** at 192 m (630 ft). At **Cap de Barbaría**, on Formentera's southern tip, you can stand on the cliff edge, with its light-house, watchtowers and Bronze Age remains, and look south to the coast of North Africa.

If you're making your own way to Formentera, rather than joining an organized excursion, then you don't need to book a return ticket. The savings are very small and you are restricted to that particular ferry line's services, when another boat may be more convenient for bringing you back. Pick up a collection of timetables for all the ferry companies at the Estación Maritima.

◀ *Formentera has many stretches of white, sandy beach*

THINGS TO SEE & DO

Ca Na Costa ★

If you're on the road from the port to Es Pujols (see page 89), take a look at what is said to be one of the most important archaeological finds in the Balearic Islands. It is a stone circle marking a megalithic burial tomb, dated to about 2000 BC. Some of the human remains, pottery and other items that were found here can be seen in the Museu Arqueològic de Dalt Vila (see page 18).

Cap de Barbaría ★

A visit to the southern tip of the island gives a glimpse of the rugged life faced by the islanders in the past. You pass through a goat-filled land-scape before finally reaching an isolated lighthouse.

La Mola ★★

The cliffs and lighthouse at the eastern tip of the island offer terrific views, not just out to sea but back over Formentera and its pinewood.

The cliffs at La Mola plunge dramatically into the sea. As there is no barrier or warning sign and nothing to break a fall, be very careful, especially with young children.

TRANSPORT

There is no airport on the island, and no plans to build one. This is part of the reason why it is so peaceful here and tourism is not on the same scale as neighbouring Ibiza. The island is tiny – only about 19 km (12 miles) long – so the best way to explore it is by bike, as you can cover most places in a day. There are specially designated cycle routes and not too many cars. Mopeds and cars can also be hired at the harbour of **La Savina**. The local bus system is erratic and cannot be relied on, but there are plenty of taxis.

SHOPPING

Apart from the shops selling local products in Sant Francesc, you will find the inevitable souvenir shops elsewhere on the island. Look out for island knitwear from the **Mercería La Mola** shop at El Pilar.

There is a daily **Hippy Market** at Es Pujols from 18.00 hours until late and in the capital, Sant Francesc, from 09.00–14.00 hours, as well as a craft market on Wednesdays and Sundays from 16.00 hours until sunset at El Pilar de la Mola.

⬥ The harbour at La Savina

Es Pujols ★★

The island's main resort is tiny by Ibizan standards but it has a decent beach and a good choice of eating places for lunch.

Las Salinas ★

Formentera's saltpans are not used now, as the salt trade has all but died out. However, they provide a good refuge for wildlife and occasionally even flamingoes have been reported there.

Sant Francesc ★★★

The island's capital is only small, but it's the best place for local souvenirs, such as knitwear, ceramics, cheese, honey and Formentera's own *hierbas* drinks. There is a small ethnological museum showing the island's history, **Museu d'Etnografia de Formentera** (ⓐ Carrer Jaume I, Sant Francesc de Formentera ❶ 971 32 26 70 ⓔ meef@cief.es ❶ Open Mon 17.00–21.00, Tues–Sat 10.00–14.00 and 17.00–21.00).

Water sports ★★

There are sailing, windsurfing and water-skiing opportunities and excellent waters for diving on the island. Ask for details at the tourist office at the port when you arrive from the ferry, or consult the free magazine, *touribisport*. Some of the beaches have pedalos. ⓦ www.touribisport.com

BEACHES

There are several excellent beaches on Formentera, and these tend to be quieter than the ones on Ibiza. The island's only real resort is at Es Pujols. **Platja de Migjorn** is popular, while **Platja de Illetes** is probably the most attractive beach.

GREEN ROUTES

A network of ancient tracks can be followed on foot or by bicycle. It forms one of the island's major attractions.

◀ *The Formentera coastline*

RESTAURANTS

For such a small island, Formentera has a wide variety of eating places specializing mainly in locally caught fish.

La Barca €€ Stylish and near the beach, with outdoor terrace. Fish and other dishes. ② Es Pujols ☏ 971 32 85 02

Bellavista €€ A good choice, right in the port of La Savina, with island food and a wider menu to cater for the tourist trade. ② Port of La Savina ☏ 971 32 22 36 🕐 Open noon–17.00 and 19.00–midnight

Can Rafalet €€ Great views from the terrace restaurant in Es Caló, in a quiet setting. A good variety of seafood, fish and rice dishes. ② Es Caló ☏ 971 32 70 77 🕐 Open 13.00–16.00 and 19.00–23.00

Pequeña Isla €€ In Es Pilar and not to be missed if you want fresh fish. Try a typical island dish such as *calamar a la Bruna* – squid fried with local sausage, potatoes and peppers. Wider menu also available. ② Es Pilar ☏ 971 32 70 68 🕐 Open 13.00–16.00 and 20.00–00.30

Restaurant Mirador € Don't miss the opportunity to stop here for a drink, snack or meal, and take in the spectacular panoramic views over the island. Ideal spot for watching the sunset. ② Es Pilar, half-way up the hill to La Mola ☏ 971 32 70 37 🕐 Open 13.00–16.00 and 19.30–23.00, 20.00–23.00 (Jul and Aug)

Tanga €€ Family-run with lobster and fish tanks. ② Right on the beach at Playa Levante ☏ 971 18 79 19 🕐 Open 09.00–20.00 (closes earlier in low season)

Food & drink

With around 2000 bars and restaurants, finding somewhere to eat and drink in Ibiza is not a problem. Deciding what to choose just might be. As well as local and Spanish food, there are also many French, Italian and Chinese restaurants. Others serve 'international' menus, including typically British dishes.

MEAL TIMES

Because Ibiza is a fishing and farming island, where people have traditionally needed to get up early, meal times are not quite as late as they are on the Spanish mainland. Lunch is usually served from about 13.30 to 15.00, with dinner from 20.00 to 23.00, but you'll always find places open if you want to eat earlier or later.

IBIZAN DISHES

Look out for typical dishes. *Sofrit pages* is made with lamb, potatoes, saffron and local sausages. *Sobrassada* (paprika-flavoured cured pork sausage) and *butiffara* (aniseed-flavoured pork sausage) are also good in a *bocadillo* (sandwich). *Guisat de peix* is a delicious fish stew usually served as two courses – first the fish with boiled potatoes and alioli (garlic mayonnaise) and then a fish soup. Naturally, fresh fish is common, but it is more expensive than other dishes. However, this is your chance to try salmon, swordfish, fresh lobsters and shellfish, at prices you would never get back home. A local favourite is squid, which doesn't appeal to everyone but is a lot tastier than you might think – a little like chicken. A way to cook it is deep-fried in batter: *calamar a la romana*.

You can't come to Spain and not try a Spanish omelette (*tortilla*) at least once. In some places an omelette is a light snack for when you're not very hungry, but the Spanish version is a meal in itself, jam-packed with potatoes and with or without onions.

◀ *Fish and seafood feature regularly on menus. Look for local wines, too*

Paella

You will see *paella* on almost every menu, so do give it a try at least once. Most places will only serve it for a minimum of two people, and to do it properly does take a little time, so be prepared to wait. Saffron rice is cooked in a big iron pan, and it's actually the pan that's the *paella*, not the food. It will have vegetables and fish thrown in, and every place has its own version. Some of the seafood *paellas* are quite spectacular to look at, with prawns, shrimps, mussels and chunks of fish. Vegetarians, take care: it's quite common to find meat in a *paella* too.

Desserts

A popular dessert is *greixonera*, a kind of bread pudding flavoured with lemon and cinnamon, and there are Ibizan versions of cheesecake (*flaó*) and crème caramel (*flan*), too, as well as plenty of fresh fruit.

DRINKS

Cervezas (Spanish beers) are widely available, and are usually slightly stronger than British beers. Wine lovers will have no shortage of choice, with good-quality Spanish wine such as Rioja, or the strong island wine called *vi pages*. *Sangria* is popular on Ibiza, but this mix of red wine, brandy, fruit juices and ice can vary from watery to having a kick like a mule. Spanish brandy isn't generally as smooth as the French version, but is a lot cheaper, while Ibiza has many liqueurs worth trying, such as *frigola* and *hierbas*, both sweet and made from herbs. If you just want a fresh fruit juice try *granizados*, served with crushed ice.

TAPAS

There are plenty of *tapas* bars around in the bigger towns, though not always in the smaller ones. The word '*tapa*' means a lid, and it comes from the custom of serving a titbit of food with a drink; the food would be placed in a saucer on top of the glass, like a lid. *Tapas* today are still nibbles, but you can make a whole meal of them if you like: seafood, chunks of meat, bits of fish, olives, salads and vegetables. If you're not sure what to ask for, go inside and just point at what you want.

◆ *Fishermen from Ibiza Town*

Menu decoder

aceitunas aliñadas Marinated olives

albóndigas en salsa Meatballs in (usually tomato) sauce

albóndigas de pescado Fish cakes

alioli Garlic-flavoured mayonnaise served as an accompaniment to just
about anything – a rice dish, vegetables, shellfish – or as a dip for bread

bistek or **biftek** Beef steak; rare is **poco hecho**, **regular** is medium and
bien hecho is well done

bocadillo The Spanish sandwich, usually made of French-style bread

caldereta Stew based on fish or lamb

caldo Soup or broth

carne Meat; **carne de ternera** is beef; **carne picada** is minced meat;
carne de cerdo is pork; **carne de cordero** is lamb

chorizo Cured, dry red-coloured sausage made from chopped pork,
paprika, spices, herbs and garlic

churros Flour fritters cooked in spiral shapes in very hot fat and cut into
strips, best dunked into hot chocolate

cordero asado Roast lamb flavoured with lemon and white wine

embutidos charcutería Pork meat preparations including **jamón** (ham),
chorizo (see above), **salchichones** (sausages) and **morcillas** (black
pudding)

ensalada Salad; the normal restaurant salad is composed of lettuce,
onion, tomato and olives

ensalada mixta As above, but with extra ingredients, such as boiled egg,
tuna fish or asparagus

escabeche Sauce of fish, meat or vegetables cooked in wine and vinegar
and left to go cold

estofado de buey Beef stew, made with carrots and turnips, or with potatoes

fiambre Any type of cold meat such as ham, **chorizo**, etc.

flan Caramel custard, the national dessert of Spain

fritura A fry up, as in **fritura de pescado** – different kinds of fried fish

gambas Prawns; **gambas a la plancha** are grilled, **gambas al ajillo** are
fried with garlic and **gambas con gabardina** deep-fried in batter

gazpacho andaluz Cold soup (originally from Andalucía) made from tomatoes, cucumbers, peppers, bread, garlic and olive oil

gazpacho manchego Hot dish made with meat (chicken or rabbit) and unleavened bread (not to be confused with **gazpacho andaluz**)

habas con jamón Broad beans fried with diced ham (sometimes with chopped hard-boiled egg and parsley)

helado Ice cream

jamón Ham; **jamón serrano** and **jamón iberico** (far more expensive) are dry cured; cooked ham is **jamón de york**

langostinos a la plancha Large prawns grilled and served with vinaigrette or **alioli**; **langostinos a la marinera** are cooked in white wine

lenguado Sole, often served cooked with wine and mushrooms

mariscos Seafood, including shellfish

menestra Dish of mixed vegetables cooked separately and combined before serving

menú del día Set menu for the day at a fixed price; it may or may not include bread, wine and a dessert, but it doesn't usually include coffee

paella Famous rice dish originally from Valencia but now made all over Spain; **paella valenciana** has chicken and rabbit; **paella de mariscos** is made with seafood; **paella mixta** combines meat and seafood

pan Bread; **pan de molde** is sliced white bread; **pan integral** wholemeal

pincho moruno Pork kebab – spicy chunks of pork on a skewer

pisto Spanish version of ratatouille, made with tomato, peppers, onions, garlic, courgette and aubergines

pollo al ajillo Chicken fried with garlic; **pollo a la cerveza** is cooked in beer; **pollo al chilindrón** is cooked with peppers, tomatoes and onions

salpicón de mariscos Seafood salad

sopa de ajo Delicious warming winter garlic soup thickened with bread, usually with a poached egg floating in it

tarta helada Popular ice-cream cake served as dessert

tortilla española Classic omelette, made with potatoes and eaten hot or cold; if you want a plain omelette ask for a **tortilla francesa**

zarzuela de pescado y mariscos Stew made with white fish and shellfish in a tomato, wine and saffron stock

LIFESTYLE

Shopping

The two most important features of recent Ibizan life, the hippy invasion and the club scene, have both had their impact on the souvenir trade too. If you want something that says 'Ibiza', check out the fashions and the jewellery. Most visitors will visit one of the hippy markets, where there is so much handmade jewellery that even the fussiest buyer should find something to appeal to themselves and their friends back home.

DRINK & TOBACCO

Although duty-free goods are no longer available in Spain, shop prices are lower here. Remember that if you buy goods in the shops, you can take home as much as you like (provided it's for your own personal

◗ *The hippy market at Es Canar*

consumption) as Spain is a fellow-member of the European Union. Peach schnapps, *hierbas* (the local herb spirit), cigarettes and many of your favourite spirits from home are cheaper here.

FASHION
Even the racks of humdrum souvenir T-shirts will include some very stylish items indeed. Ibiza Town is the place to head to hunt out fashion designs. A T-shirt from one of the renowned clubs will go down very well with youngsters at home. The major clubs have their own shops in the port in Ibiza. Spanish chains like Mango and Zara are much cheaper for women's fashion than at home.

LEATHER GOODS
Sandals, shoes, bags, wallets, and other leather and suede goods are generally well made and reasonably priced. Lots of the souvenir shops sell them, and many places have their own specialist shop with a resident leather-worker.

POTTERY
You'll be amazed at the variety of pottery that's for sale on Ibiza, and even more amazed when you realize that no clay is available on the island. Clay is imported from mainland Spain and fired on Ibiza, but a lot of stuff is also imported and then sold as if it had been made here. Buy something because you like it and not because you have to have something made locally. Having said that, there are many local potters producing good work in their own workshops, while if you drive around you're sure to see lots of ceramic 'superstores' (looking a bit like garden centres) by the side of the road. These sell everything from thimbles to huge plant pots.

OPENING TIMES
Department stores and hypermarkets normally open from 09.00 to 23.00, while smaller shops are open from 09.00 to 13.30 and again from 17.00 to 20.00 or 22.00 in the high season.

LIFESTYLE

Kids

Although Ibiza attracts a lot of publicity for its club scene, it is still the perfect place for a family holiday if you choose the right resort. Many hotels provide organized children's clubs and activities. Even if they don't, there is likely to be a games room or swimming pool for the youngsters.

BOATS
Plenty of places also have glass-bottomed boats (Sant Antoni even has a glass-bottomed catamaran!) to take you out to look at the wildlife under the sea, and the Es Canar trip includes a look at a sunken ship for good measure.

GO-KARTS
There are several go-kart tracks, including one near Sant Antoni, and one between Ibiza Town and Santa Eulària which has baby karts.
ⓘ 971 34 38 05/971 31 77 44

TRAINS
Several resorts (Es Canar, Portinatx, Santa Eulària and Sant Antoni among them) have miniature trains that chug along the coast and into the countryside for an hour or so, usually with a free drink for everyone half-way around.

WATER PARK
Aguamar Water Park is well worth a day out. ⓐ Platja d'en Bossa
ⓘ 971 39 67 90 ⓒ Open daily in summer 10.00–18.00

WATER SPORTS
It's a very small beach indeed that doesn't offer a few facilities, such as pedalos for hire, while older children might like to take lessons in wind-surfing, available on most larger beaches.

▶ *A water park is a good place to spend the day*

Sports & activities

In Ibiza you can do nothing all day if you wish, just turning over every once in a while to keep the tan even. You can exert all your night-time energies in the clubs. But if it's more conventional holiday activity you're after, then Ibiza has plenty of that too.

CYCLING

Tourist information offices can provide a leaflet covering the island's mountain-biking routes, and bikes can be hired in almost every holiday resort. Ibiza's neighbour, Formentera, is great for both walking and cycling – you can rent bikes right outside the ferry terminal.

DIVING

Ibiza has some of the cleanest waters in the Mediterranean, which makes for great diving with clear visibility. Explore submarine caves and a world of corals, colourful fish and sea anemones. Contact your local tourist office for information, ask at your hotel reception.

GO-KARTING

A go-kart track at **Santa Eulària** offers thrills by day and night and even has baby karts for kids. ❶ 971 31 77 44 ❿ www.gokartssantaeulalia.com

GOLF

There's a golf course at **Roca Llisa** which in fact is two courses in one, with separate 9- and 18-hole courses. ❷ On the coast midway between Ibiza Town and Santa Eulària ❶ 971 19 61 18 ❸ golfibiza@retemail.com

INDOOR SPORTS

In addition to facilities in some of the larger hotels, there are two municipal sports centres offering badminton, squash and indoor tennis and indoor/outdoor swimming pools among other activities.
Polideportivo Municipal de Eivissa ⓐ Ibiza Town ❶ 971 31 35 64
Polideportivo Municipal de Sant Antoni ⓐ Sant Antoni ❶ 971 34 54 02

RIDING

There are numerous stables on the island, including:

Finca Can Puig ⓐ Santa Gertrudis ⓣ 600 05 93 43
Can Mayans ⓐ Santa Eulària ⓣ 971 18 73 88
Easy Rider ⓐ Cala Llonga ⓣ 971 19 65 11

There are others at Sant Antoni and Sant Llorenç.as well.

SAILING

Ibiza is a haven for yachts, with several thousand moorings. There are sailing schools in Ibiza Town, Santa Eulària, Sant Antoni and at many of the beaches. Throughout the year there are regattas, races and competitions for sailors. There are sailing schools on several beaches in Ibiza and Formentera. Check with your tourist office or hotel.

WALKING

There are several way-marked trails starting from popular tourist spots in various parts of the island, such as Santa Eulària, Sant Antoni, Platja d'en Bossa and Sant Miquel. Known as 'Falcon Routes', these trails may lead to charming villages, secluded beaches or along dramatic clifftops. All routes are well signposted with the symbol of a falcon, and at the start of the trails there is a board indicating the route and the level of difficulty. You can get leaflets from the tourist information office in Ibiza Town, in Sant Antoni or Santa Eulària.

WATER SPORTS

Nowhere on Ibiza is more than a few miles from the sea. Most of the main beaches have some water sports facilities, ranging from the basic pedalos and boats for hire through to more sophisticated options. The law in Spain requires you to have an official licence in order to take charge of a motor boat, so you're unlikely to be given this choice.

There are at least 20 places with windsurfing equipment for hire, with well-established schools in Platja d'en Bossa and Santa Eulària. During the summer season, the winds are ideal for beginners; in the autumn they become stronger.

Festivals & events

ART

Numerous artists have settled on, or visited, Ibiza over the years and as a result there is a flourishing contemporary art scene. A stroll around Ibiza Town will show you some of its many galleries, and you might also want to visit the **Museu d'Art Contemporani (Museum of Contemporary Art)** on the Ronda Narcis Puget in the Dalt Vila (see page 18). There is also a small art scene in Santa Gertrudis, with a couple of galleries there too.

DANCING

Many hotels and restaurants put on flamenco displays, though flamenco is gypsy dancing from mainland Andalucía and not an Ibizan tradition. The island's dance is called *ball pages* and is thought to be at least 3000 years old, having started as a pagan fertility dance. You can see it performed, and explained, every Thursday at about 18.00 in front of the church at **Sant Miquel** (the inland village and not the beach resort). There is also a small craft market from 18.00–22.00.

FESTIVALS

If you hear of a festival (*fiesta*) in your resort, or at a nearby church or village, do make an effort to go along as you'll be made very welcome. People will appreciate you showing an interest in their culture and you'll see a slice of real Ibizan life.

During the summer season there's the flower festival in Santa Eulària on the first Sunday in May, and a medieval festival in Dalt Vila on the second weekend in May, celebrating the declaration of Eivissa as a World Heritage Site. The Festival of Sant Joan is on 24 June. This is celebrated with bonfires and fireworks not only in the village of Sant Joan but elsewhere.

On 16 July is the Festival of Our Lady of Carmen, who is the patron saint of sailors: boats are paraded and blessed, especially in Ibiza Town.

◀ *Flamenco dancers*

On 25 July is the feast of San Jaime, the patron saint of Formentera.

From 1 to 8 August are the Festival of the Earth, 'Festes de la Terra'; the Festival of Our Lady of the Snows, the patron saint of these Pine Islands; and the Festival of San Ciriaco, patron saint of Ibiza Town. Needless to say, this develops into one long party, culminating in a firework display.

The final two big summer festivals are on 24 August (Festival of Sant Bartolomeu, in Sant Antoni) with fireworks and music, and 8 September (Fiesta of Jesús, in Santa Eulària), a religious festival with traditional dance.

The Tourist Day

Every year in October there is a Tourist Festival. Hotels and town halls arrange special dances and food tasting. Ask for further information at the tourist offices.

◐ *Local festivals provide colour and interest*

Preparing to go

GETTING THERE

The cheapest way to get to Ibiza is to book a package holiday with one of the leading tour operators specializing in Ibiza holidays. You should also check the travel supplements of the weekend newspapers, such as the *Sunday Telegraph*, and *The Sunday Times*. The internet is obviously a good source of information for holidays to the island.

If your travelling times are flexible, and if you can avoid the school holidays, you can also find some very cheap last-minute deals using the websites of the leading holiday companies.

BEFORE YOU LEAVE

Holidays should be about fun and relaxation, so avoid last-minute panics and stress by making your preparations well in advance.

It is not necessary to have inoculations to travel in Europe, but you should make sure you and your family are up to date with the basics, such as tetanus. It is a good idea to pack a small first-aid kit to carry with you containing plasters, antiseptic cream, travel sickness pills, insect repellent and/or bite relief cream, antihistamine tablets, upset stomach remedies and painkillers. Sun lotion can be more expensive in Ibiza than in the UK so it is worth taking a good selection especially of the higher-factor lotions if you have children with you, and don't forget after-sun cream as well. If you are taking prescription medicines, ensure that you take enough for the duration of your visit – you may find it impossible to obtain the same medicines in Ibiza. It is also worth having a dental check-up before you go.

DOCUMENTS

The most important documents you will need are your tickets and your passport. Check well in advance that your passport is up to date and has at least three months left to run (six months is even better). All children, including newborn babies, need their own passport now, unless they are already included on the passport of the person they are travelling with. It generally takes at least three weeks to process a passport renewal. This can be longer in the run-up to the summer months. For the latest information on how to renew your passport and the processing times call the Passport Agency on ☎ 0870 521 0410, or access their website Ⓦ www.ukpa.gov.uk

You should check the details of your travel tickets well before your departure, ensuring that the timings and dates are correct.

If you are thinking of hiring a car while you are away, you will need to have your UK driving licence with you. If you want more than one driver for the car, the other drivers must have their licences too.

MONEY

Cashpoints are found throughout Ibiza and Formentera, but you may have to travel to find one if you are staying in a quiet beach area. It is no longer necessary to bring travellers' cheques with you. To buy travellers' cheques or exchange money at a bank you may need to give up to a week's notice, depending on the quantity of foreign currency you require. You can exchange money at the airport before you depart. You should also make sure that your credit, charge and debit cards are up to date – you do not want them to expire mid-holiday – and that your credit limit is sufficient to allow you to make those holiday purchases. Don't forget, too, to check your PIN numbers in case you haven't used them for a while – you may want to draw money from cash dispensers while you are away. Ring your bank or card company and they will help you out.

INSURANCE

Do you have sufficient cover for your holiday? Check that your policy covers you adequately for loss of possessions and valuables, for activities you might want to try – such as scuba-diving, horse-riding, or water sports – and for emergency medical and dental treatment, including flights home, if required.

After January 2006, a new EHIC card replaces the E111 form to allow UK visitors access to reduced-cost, and sometimes free state-provided medical treatment in the EEA. For further information, ring EHIC enquiries line: ☎ 0845 605 0707, or visit the Department of Health website ⓦ www.dh.gov.uk

CLIMATE

Summers are warm and winters are mild. Summer clothing is advisable although a light jacket is recommended in the early hours due to the humidity of the island. From September on, a raincoat is a good idea in case of autumn storms, which last only a few hours.

PETS

Remember to make arrangements for the care of your pets while you are away – book them into a reputable cat or dog hotel, or make arrangements with a trustworthy neighbour to ensure that they are properly fed, watered and exercised while you are on holiday.

SECURITY

Take precautions to prevent your house being burgled while you are away.

- Cancel milk, newspapers and other regular deliveries so that post and milk does not pile up on the doorstep, indicating that you are away.
- Let the postman know where to leave parcels and bulky mail that will not go through your letterbox – ideally with a next-door neighbour.
- If possible, arrange for a friend or neighbour to visit regularly, closing and opening curtains in the evening and morning, and switching lights on and off to give the impression that the house is being lived in.
- Consider buying electrical timing devices that will switch lights and radios on and off, again to give the impression that there is someone in the house.
- Let Neighbourhood Watch representatives know that you will be away so that they can keep an eye on your home.

◀ *Springtime in Ibiza*

- If you have a burglar alarm, make sure that it is serviced and working properly and is switched on when you leave (you may find that your insurance policy requires this). Ensure that a neighbour is able to gain access to the alarm to turn it off if it is triggered accidentally.
- If you are leaving cars unattended, put them in a garage, if possible, and leave a key with a neighbour in case the alarm goes off.

AIRPORT PARKING & ACCOMMODATION

If you intend to leave your car in an airport car park while you are away, or stay the night at an airport hotel before or after your flight, you should book well ahead to take advantage of discounts or cheap off-airport parking. Airport accommodation gets booked up several weeks in advance, especially during the height of the holiday season. Check whether the hotel offers free parking for the duration of the holiday – often the savings made can significantly reduce the price.

PACKING TIPS

Baggage allowances vary according to the airline, destination and the class of travel, but 20 kg (44 lb) per person is the norm for luggage that is carried in the hold (it usually tells you what the weight limit is on your ticket). You are also allowed one item of cabin baggage weighing no more than 5 kg (11 lb), and measuring 46 by 30 by 23 cm (18 by 12 by 9 inches). In addition, you can usually carry your airport purchases, as well as umbrella, handbag, coat, camera, etc., as hand baggage. Large items – surfboards, golf-clubs, collapsible wheelchairs and pushchairs – are usually charged as extras and it is a good idea to let the airline know in advance that you want to bring these.

TELEPHONING IBIZA

To call Ibiza from the UK, dial 00 34 followed by the nine-digit number – there's no need to wait for a dialling tone.

CHECK-IN, PASSPORT CONTROL & CUSTOMS

First-time travellers can often find airport security intimidating, but it is all very easy really.

- Check-in desks usually open two or three hours before the flight is due to depart. Arrive early for the best choice of seats.
- Look for your flight number on the TV monitors in the check-in area, and find the relevant check-in desk. Your tickets will be checked and your luggage taken. Take your boarding card and go to the departure gate. Here your hand luggage will be X-rayed and your passport checked.
- In the departure area, you can shop and relax, but watch the monitors that tell you when to board – usually about 30 minutes before take-off. Go to the departure gate shown on the monitor and follow the instructions given to you by the airline staff.

During your stay

AIRPORTS

Ibiza has only one airport, which is located 8 km (5 miles) away from Ibiza Town. Because the island is so small, it is only an hour's drive to any resort. ℹ 971 80 91 32

The majority of visitors use charter companies to get to Ibiza, which operate from nearly all of the UK's regional airports. Ibiza's modern airport is also served by scheduled international flights from the UK and by internal flights from Spanish airports at Madrid, Valencia and Barcelona. Car hire is available (best booked in advance from home) along with taxis. If you are on a package holiday, airport transfers are likely to be included.

BEACHES

During summer, many beaches have life-guards and a flag safety system. Make sure that you are fully familiar with the flag system for Ibiza. Other, quieter, beaches may be safe for swimming but there are unlikely to be life-guards or life-saving amenities available. Bear in mind that the strong winds that develop in the hotter months can quickly change a

BEACH SAFETY

Most beaches where the public bathe in numbers operate a flag system to indicate the sea conditions.

● Red (or black) flag: dangerous – no swimming.

● Yellow: good swimmers only – apply caution.

● Green (or white): safe bathing conditions for all.

safe beach into a not-so-safe one, and that some can have strong currents the further out you go. If in doubt, ask your local holiday representative or enquire at your hotel. (See above for details of Beach Safety flag warnings.)

CHILDREN'S ACTIVITIES

Go-Karts On the road from Sant Antoni to Ibiza Town, 14 km (8.7 miles). ❶ 971 34 38 05 ● Open 10.00–midnight

Karting Santa Eulària On the road from Ibiza Town to Santa Eulària, 6 km (3.6 miles). ❶ 971 31 77 44 ● Open 10.00–20.30

La Huerta A special place to enjoy a day in the country. See local animals, ride a horse, donkey or pony. Sample speciality foods at the bar-and-grill restaurant and enjoy the swimming pool, solarium, mini-golf, volleyball and children's park. ❸ On the road from Santa Gertrudis to San Lorenzo ❶ 646 488 048 ● Open 10.00–18.00

Aquarium Cap Blanca Special boat trips from Sant Antoni's harbour. ❸ In Cala Gracio, 1.5 km (0.9 miles) away from Sant Antoni ❶ 650 26 58 22 Ⓦ www.aquariumcapblanca.com ● Open 10.30–18.30

Can Marça Caves Forty-minute guided tour. ❸ In Port de Sant Miquel ● Open 10.00–20.00

Ibiza en Globo This is Ibiza from a balloon. ❶ 630 41 01 67 Ⓦ www.ibizaenglobo.com

Bowling Centre Bowling, mini-golf and trampolines. ❸ Carrer Murta 2–4 ❶ 971 39 03 56

CHURCHES

Churches normally have a service in the morning and another in the evening. Check times at the reception of your hotel, at the local newspaper or in the tourist office.

CONSULATE

British Vice-Consulate ❷ Avenida Isidoro Macabich 45, 1st floor, 07800 Ibiza ❶ 971 30 18 18

The Irish Consulate ❸ Carrer Sant Miquel 68 A, 07002 Palma de Mallorca ❶ 971 71 92 44

CURRENCY

Currency In line with the majority of EU member states, Spain entered the single currency on 1 Jan 2002. Euro note denominations are 500, 200, 100, 50, 20, 10 and 5. Coins are 1 and 2 euros and 1, 2, 5, 10, 20 and 50 céntimos.

Changing money You can change travellers' cheques and sterling at any bank, or at travel agencies, exchange bureaux, larger hotels and some shops, although banks give better rates. Look for the *Cambio* sign. You will need your passport when cashing travellers' cheques, but not for changing cash.

Banks Cashpoints are found throughout the islands and dispense money day and night. 🕐 Open normally Mon–Fri 08.30 to 14.00

Credit cards Widely used in the tourist resorts, and can be used as a deposit on car hire. If you run short of cash you may be able to get money on your credit card at one of the major banks, or at a cashpoint.

ELECTRICITY

Electricity is 220V all over the island and 2-pin plugs are used. Adaptors can be found both in hotel receptions and in souvenirs shops.

If you are considering buying electrical appliances to take home, always check that they will work in the UK before you buy.

FACILITIES FOR THE DISABLED

Wheelchairs can be rented in **Ortofarma Tur Viñas**, Ibiza Town
(📍 Avenida España 6 ☎ 971 39 28 91 🕐 Mon–Sat 10.00–13.30 and
17.00–21.00). Electric wheelchairs can be hired from **Farmàcia
Ramia-Planas** (📍 Av. España 36 ☎ 971 30 13 79).

GETTING AROUND

Car hire and driving Car hire is a popular way of getting around the
island, and rates are very competitive. You can rent a car by the day,
which usually means that you've got it for 24 hours. Your holiday rep
may be the best person to help with arrangements.

Spain has one of the worst records for road accidents in Europe, so
do take care and don't take chances. As a foreigner in a hired car you will
probably get the blame for any accident, so you may want to consider
paying that little bit extra for full insurance.

There are mopeds and motorbikes for hire in all the main resorts, and
they are a cheap way of getting to out-of-the-way beaches. Accidents
happen, though, so take care. If you're 16 or over you can rent a machine
under 49 cc – you have to be 18 to get one that's 75 cc or over. Crash
helmets are compulsory, and ensure you have adequate insurance cover.

Public transport The good news is that buses on Ibiza are very cheap
and can probably get you to most places you would want to go to on the
island. The bad news is that some can be crowded. Ibiza Town is the hub
and the bus station is on Avenida Isidoro Macabich. 🌐 www.ibizabus.com

> ### ROAD RULES
> Speed limits are: 50 km/h (37 mph) in towns, 90 km/h (57 mph)
> outside, unless otherwise marked. Spanish police often mount
> speed traps and have the power to make on-the-spot fines.

⊙ *There are plenty of ways of getting around*

Boats In Sant Antoni and Ibiza Town you can hop on a boat that goes to just about any of the nearby beaches. There are regular ferries from Ibiza Town across to the Spanish mainland, to Palma de Mallorca and to the neighbouring island of Formentera, a popular day trip (see page 85).

Taxis The sticker saying SP on the front and back bumpers doesn't mean Spain, it means *Servicio Público*, or public service vehicle. A green light on the roof above the driver's seat means the taxi is for hire. You can usually find a list of the fixed prices attached to a post next to the taxi rank, to give you a guideline. A 10 per cent tip is about right. All taxi drivers have a permit number, so make a note of it in the unlikely event of any disagreement, in which case a ticket will be needed.

Ferries If you have the time you can travel to Ibiza from Barcelona, Valencia, Denia or Palma de Mallorca on one of the ferries operated by **Trasmediterranea** (W www.trasmediterranea.es), whose UK agent is **Southern Ferries** (3 30 Churton Street, London SW1V 2LP ❶ 0870 499 1305 W www.southernferries.co.uk). Early bookings are necessary for school holidays, and pensioners get a 20 per cent discount.

HEALTH MATTERS

Sunburn Avoid sun exposure between 13.00 and 16.00 hours, and use high SPF sun lotions in order to prevent sunburn, especially in children.

Pharmacies One of the *farmàcias* (pharmacies) is always on duty, with the details displayed at all other pharmacies. Look for the red or green cross. Pharmacists are trained to deal with minor medical problems, and in most places speak good English.

Medical care Seek help from your hotel or holiday rep if you need medical care. For emergencies, there is a 24-hour outpatient service at the main hospital, **Hospital Can Misses** (❶ 971 39 70 00), in Ibiza Town, and there are several other outpatient services at smaller hospitals around the island. All the large resorts have a *médico* (resident doctor).

THE LANGUAGE

The Ibicencos respond warmly to visitors who attempt to speak a little of their language. Here are a few words and phrases to get you started:

ENGLISH	SPANISH (pronunciation)
General vocabulary	
yes	*sí* (see)
no	*no* (no)
please	*por favor* (por faBOR)
thank you (very much)	*(muchas) gracias* ((MOOchas) GRAtheeyas)
You're welcome	*de nada* (deNAda)
hello	*hola* (Ola)
goodbye	*adiós* (adeeYOS)
good morning/day	*buenos días* (BWEnos DEEyas)
good afternoon/evening	*buenas tardes* (BWEnas TARdes)
good evening (after dark)	*buenas noches* (BWEnas NOches)
excuse me (to get attention or to get past)	*¡disculpe!* (desKOOLpay)
excuse me (to apologize or to ask pardon)	*¡perdón!* (perDON)
Sorry	*lo siento* (lo seeYENtoe)
Help!	*¡socorro!* (SOHcohroe)
today	*hoy* (oy)
tomorrow	*mañana* (manYAna)
yesterday	*ayer* (ayYER)
Useful words and phrases	
open	*abierto* (abeeYERtoe)
closed	*cerrado* (therRAdoe)
push	*empujar* (empooHAR)
pull	*tirar* (teeRAR)
How much is it?	*¿Cuánto es?* (KWANtoe es)
bank	*el banco* (el BANko)

ENGLISH	SPANISH (pronunciation)

Useful words and phrases (continued)

ENGLISH	SPANISH (pronunciation)
bureau de change	*la oficina de cambio* (la ofeeTHEEna de KAMbeeyo)
post office	*correos* (koRAYos)
duty (all-night) chemist	*la farmàcia de guardia* (la farMAHtheeya de garDEEya)
bank card	*la tarjeta de banco* (la tarHEHta de BANko)
credit card	*la tarjeta de crédito* (la tarHEHta de CREdeetoe)
travellers' cheques	*los cheques de viaje* (los CHEkes de beeAhay)
menu	*el menú/la carta* (el menOO/la KARta)
waiter	*el/la camarero/a* (el/la kahmahRERo/a)
water	*agua* (Agwa)
fizzy/still water	*agua con/sin gas* (Agwa con/sin gas)
I don't understand	*no entiendo* (No enteeYENdoe)
The bill, please	*La cuenta, por favor* (la KWENta, porfaBOR)
Do you speak English?	*¿Habla usted inglés?* (Ablah OOsted eenGLES)
My name is ...	*Me llamo ...* (meh YAmoh ...)
Where are the toilets?	*¿Dónde están los servicios?* (DONdeh esTAN os serBEEtheeos)
Where is there a telephone?	*¿Dónde está un teléfono?* (DONdeh esTAH oon teLEfono)
Can you call me a taxi?	*¿Puede llamar a un taxi?* (PWEday yaMAR ah oon TAKsee)
Can you help me?	*¿Puede ayudarme?* (PWEday ayooDARmeh)

MEDIA

International newspapers are available in Ibiza Town and some resorts. The local newspapers are **Diario de Ibiza** (Ⓦ www.diariodeibiza.es) and **Ultima Hora de Ibiza y Formentera** (Ⓦ www.ultimahora.es/ibiza).

WHAT TO DO IN AN EMERGENCY

If your holiday rep is not available to help, then the following phone numbers may be useful:

Emergency services	112
National Police	091
Local Police	092
Guardia Civil	062

PERSONAL COMFORT AND SECURITY

Most hotels offer laundry services – ask at reception. There are several laundries and launderettes on Ibiza; ask for *Lavandería* at tourist offices.

In Ibiza Town the only public toilets are in the old town, Dalt Vila, in Santa Lucia Bastion. Otherwise it is advisable to go into a bar or coffee shop and buy a bottle of water or a coffee.

Complaints can be made directly at the hotel reception, in the establishment that the complaint is about or at the several tourist offices.

A free special quick-dial number (☎ 112), gives direct access to all the emergency services: ambulance, fire and police.

Crime prevention Crime is not a major problem by any means, but watch out for pickpockets and bag-snatchers in markets, bus stations and other crowded places. Don't take anything valuable to the beach or leave it lying around when you go for a swim. Likewise, if you hire a car, try not to leave any bags where people can see them. There is also a small drugs problem on Ibiza, and occasional muggings have happened by people desperate for money. Try not to be on your own late at night. It is also illegal for flowers or tickets to be sold in the street and do not be tempted by games in the street, they are rigged!

Lost property If you lose something then report it to the police or the *Guardia Civil* (Civil Guard). The vast majority of Ibicencos are honest and will hand in any lost property. If you have children and one of them wanders away from you, just ask for help in the nearest bar, restaurant, hotel or shop, or go to the nearest police or *Guardia Civil* station, which is where lost children should be taken.

POST OFFICES

Post offices are normally 🕐 Mon–Fri 08.30–20.30 and Sat 08.30–13.00; there are main post offices in Ibiza Town, Sant Antoni and Santa Eulària (look for the Correos sign). Elsewhere you can often buy stamps at tobacconists (look for the Tabacos sign). Official post boxes are a distinctive yellow, but remember that most hotel receptions will send cards for you. Allow up to a week for your postcards to get home.

TELEPHONES

Public telephones work well, and usually have instructions in several languages. Stock up with coins or, much easier, buy a phonecard for 6 euros or 12 euros at a *Tabacos* (tobacconist), a shop or a hotel. Lots of bars and restaurants also have pay phones. In some resorts there special telephone shops where you can make your call, local or international, and pay for it afterwards. Internet facilities are also available.

To make a local call, ring the nine-figure number listed. All numbers throughout the Balearic Islands are prefixed with the code **971**. If you want to use your mobile phone while on holiday, check with your provider for international roaming set-up and rates.

TIME DIFFERENCES

The time in Ibiza is the same as in the Iberian Peninsula, that is, one hour ahead of Greenwich Mean Time.

PHONING ABROAD

To call an overseas number, dial **00** (the international access code), then the country code (UK = **44**), then the area code (minus the initial 0), then the number.

TIPPING

How much and whether to tip is entirely a matter of personal choice.

TOURIST OFFICES

Ibiza Town Oficina d'Informació Turistica

ⓐ Antonio Riquer 2, Puerto de Ibiza

ⓣ 971 30 19 00

ⓦ www.visitbalears.com

ⓛ Mon–Fri 09.30–13.30 and 17.00–19.30 and Sat 10.30–13.00

Vara de Rey information point

ⓐ Opposite Hotel Montesol, Ibiza Town

ⓣ 971 19 43 93

ⓛ Mon–Fri 09.00–14.00 and 16.00–21.00

Sant Antoni de Portmany

ⓐ Passeig de Ses Fonts, s/n

ⓣ 971 34 01 11   ⓦ www.santantoni.net

ⓛ Mon–Fri 09.30–20.30 and Sat–Sun 09.30–13.30

Santa Eulària des Riu

ⓐ Carrer Mariano Riquer 4

ⓣ 971 33 07 28   ⓦ www.santaeulalia.net

ⓛ Mon–Fri 09.30–13.30 and 17.00–19.30, Sat 09.30–13.30

There are some Information Points in the main square (S'Alamera), Cala Llonga and Es Canar too.

Formentera

ⓐ 07870 Port de la Savina

ⓣ 971 32 20 57   ⓦ www.illadeformentera.com and www.visitbalears.com

ⓛ Mon–Fri 10.00–14.00 and 17.00–19.00, Sat 10.00–14.00

USEFUL WEBSITES

www.ibiza.com Well-presented site about island life and culture.
www.sortmyibiza.co.uk Comprehensive directory.
www.world-guides.com Tourist guide, including weather and tips.
www.ibiza-spotlight.com Selection of hotels, shops and businesses
of interest to the tourist.

WATER

The Balearic Islands enjoy a Mediterranean climate characterized by long
periods of drought. It is, therefore, important to conserve such a scarce
natural asset. It is recommended that only the necessary amount of
water be used at all times.

WEIGHTS & MEASURES

The official units of weights and measures are the kilo and the gram.
All produce is sold like this.

Bars and restaurants here do not sell spirits, beers or wine according
to official guidelines, so be careful, as you may find that a measure of
whisky, for example, is much larger than the one you would receive back
at home. Normally, the bartenders just pour until the glass is nearly full
and then add a splash of the mixer of your choice!

Imperial to metric	Metric to imperial
1 inch = 2.54 centimetres	1 centimetre = 0.4 inches
1 foot = 30 centimetres	1 metre = 3 feet, 3 inches
1 mile = 1.6 kilometres	1 kilometre = 0.6 miles
1 ounce = 28 grams	1 gram = 0.04 ounces
1 pound = 454 grams	1 kilogram = 2.2 pounds
1 pint = 0.6 litres	1 litre = 1.8 pints
1 gallon = 4.6 litres	

INDEX

ACKNOWLEDGEMENTS

We would like to thank all the photographers, picture libraries and organisations for the loan of the photographs reproduced in this book, to whom copyright in the photograph belongs:
Mike Gerrard (pages 19 and 79); Jupiter Images Corporation (pages 107, 125); Malou/Pacha (page 68); Pictures Colour Library Ltd (pages 29, 34, 81, 82, 95); Juliet Roddy-Stevenson (pages 44, 55, 62, 84, 88, 117); Thomas Cook Tour Operations Ltd (pages 1, 5, 11, 13, 16, 20, 25, 26, 31, 37, 40, 43, 49, 52, 56, 64, 58, 61, 71, 72, 75, 76, 87, 91, 92, 94, 98, 101, 104, 106); Geoff Williamson Image Collection (pages 23, 110).

We would also like to thank the following for their contribution to this series:
John Woodcock (map and symbols artwork);
Becky Alexander, Patricia Baker, Sophie Bevan, Judith Chamberlain-Webber, Stephanie Evans, Nicky Gyopari, Krystyna Mayer, Robin Pridy (editorial support); Christine Engert, Suzie Johanson, Richard Lloyd, Richard Peters, Alistair Plumb, Jane Prior, Barbara Theisen, Ginny Zeal, Barbara Zuñiga (design support).

Send your thoughts to
books@thomascook.com

- Found a beach bar, peaceful stretch of sand or must-see sight that we don't feature?

- Like to tip us off about any information that needs a little updating?

- Want to tell us what you love about this handy, little guidebook and more importantly how we can make it even handier?

Then here's your chance to tell all! Send us ideas, discoveries and recommendations today and then look out for your valuable input in the next edition of this title. And, as an extra 'thank you' from Thomas Cook Publishing, you'll be automatically entered into our exciting monthly prize draw.

Send an email to the above address or write to:
HotSpots Project Editor, Thomas Cook Publishing, PO Box 227, Unit 15/16, Coningsby Road, Peterborough PE3 8SB, UK